Thies Böttcher

Gentle Horse Training

A new four-step approach
for horse and rider

Gentle Horse Training

A new four-step approach for horse and rider

Thies Böttcher

CADMOS

Imprint

Copyright © 2010 by Cadmos Verlag Schwarzenbek
Design and setting: Ravenstein + Partner, Verden
Cover photo: Jochen Becker
Photography unless otherwise indicated: Jochen Becker
Editor: Cora von Hindte
Translation: Claire Williams
Printed by: Westermann Druck, Zwickau

British Library Cataloguing in Publication Data: A catalogue record of this book is available from the British Library.

Printed in Germany

ISBN 978-3-86127-977-8

Contents

The first steps

Foreword: The first steps

'Was that my fault again, or does my horse just not want to do it?'

Which of us hasn't thought this before? This question is always with us whatever we do and everywhere we go. It either makes us annoyed with our horses or frustrated with ourselves because we should be able to do it by now. And we have actually got it right before...

But should we even be asking ourselves this question – doesn't it assume that the horse knows exactly what he should be doing? Where does this knowledge come from? Is the horse genetically programmed to understand what the leg aids mean and how to carry someone on its back? These considerations are just too nonsensical to deserve any further thought. It is up to us to teach the horse how to do the things that we want him to do – not the actual movements such as walking or trotting of course, but rather to do these movements when we ask him by using our aids. When it comes to a fully trained horse, then the above question is appropriate – but, hand on heart, which of us owns such a horse? And who is responsible for keeping him like that?

One of the basic problems in all spheres of riding is that only a minority of horses are actually fully trained. Despite this we try to ride them as if they are. Whether you like it or not, as soon as your horse isn't ridden by a true professional, you become your own horse's trainer. As a result of this responsibility arises one question: How do I tell my horse what I would like him to do? Automatically following on from this comes the question: What exactly am I supposed to explain?

My role as a course leader has had a great influence on the choice of the exercises I use in this book. There is a huge difference between working with someone constantly over weeks and months and working with a wide range of horse and rider combinations during a weekend course. Techniques that you use in a shorter training course must be easy to understand and quick to apply for as many of the participants as possible because further assistance can, if ever, only be given at the next training session. In this respect, it is worth considering how to structure the training so that the horse can discover what he is supposed to. In my opinion the same applies to training books. Just as I don't know who is going to come to one of my courses, I don't know who will read my book. At least during a clinic I can see the participants and can ride the horses and thus judge better where a problem may lie and adjust my training accordingly. Against this background the order of each of the individual exercises is important. They go from easy to difficult and the warm-ups often act as corrections for the exercises to follow.

And so we start along an exciting path – it is no longer a question of English or Western riding styles, who is to blame, or similar issues. Instead, learning behaviour, psychology and the sequence in which the movements are carried out take centre stage. Let's just see where it takes us.

Thies Böttcher

Basic principles

Everyone has their own idea of the perfect horse. Reality, admittedly, often looks quite different because your own horse generally can't read your mind. Training, or rather education, consists of communicating our point of view to our horse. So let's first take five minutes out to establish what this picture of the perfect horse might look like – draw your own picture in your mind's eye. It is important to look for specific things. Clichés like 'a partner', 'well behaved' or 'trusting' may sound good but how do you get a horse to meet these criteria?

The background to my own picture consists of three 'primary colours': movement, distance and softness. It is always these things that cause people and their horses the most problems.

Movement

One of my most interesting horses awaited me in the form of a nine-year-old quarter horse gelding. According to his owner, 'After warming up he won't go forwards!' We quickly arranged a day and time, and when I arrived she and her saddled horse were waiting for me in the indoor school. The saddle had already been checked and the vet had visited, so we knew that neither the saddle nor the horse's back were an issue.

While he was being worked in Jet, as the horse was called, went well. The surprise came as I asked his owner to take up more of a contact and start to work with more bend. In the middle of a 10-metre circle Jet turned in and stopped. It was impossible to get the horse to move from the spot. I hadn't expected that 'not moving forwards' was meant literally! His owner explained that using a whip or spurs only caused him to either rear or buck.

Taking my courage in my own hands I got on the horse and began to use my 'standard trick' – if a horse won't go forwards then he has to go sideways or backwards. Stepping sideways is an especially effective method to get a horse to move without having to get too heavy or rough. This time it failed completely. It wasn't even possible to move the horse's hips over using my leg in order to cause some sort of movement.

The only allowance the horse made was to give slightly through his neck to the right and left. By quickly moving a horse's neck from side to side you can often unbalance them and thus get some sort of movement – not with Jet, though.

A break to contemplate our options was called for. Given that every living creature learns from any given situation, we had to create an environment in which movement was more pleasant than standing still. My method would have to use the horse's own mind – he had to decide that he wanted to move. Any attempt to try and force the horse to move could only end in failure.

The solution lay in making standing still uncomfortable for Jet, without getting rough or forcing him to defend himself. I took up the right rein so that the horse's head was held at a right angle to his body and waited. Owing to the bend in his neck the horse is no longer able to stand in balance, and his neck muscles start to get tired.

After about five minutes Jet started to get uncomfortable, having already tried to straighten his head. Winding the rein once around the saddle horn ensured that he couldn't pull the reins out of my hand. It was easy enough though to unwind the reins quickly if the situation required him to have his head. The safety of both horse and rider should always take top priority.

What started as fidgeting led to Jet moving his right leg to correct his balance.

I immediately loosened the rein and praised him. Over the next few minutes he realised that his movement had released him from an uncomfortable position. After a further five minutes spent hobbling around – taking up the reins repeatedly led him to momentary movement – you could see that he began to move forwards consistently.

Believe me, there is no funnier picture than a rider on a horse that doesn't want to move – but only when you are a spectator of course.

Training must always take into consideration the horse's nature. Movement is an essential element of this.
(Photo: Slawik)

It's an easy calculation: 600 kilograms on four legs. If we want to do something even with only one (!) leg, we are not going to be able to move the required 150 kilograms physically. Therefore the horse has to be the one to move himself and lift his leg – only then are we able to have any influence on the movement and steer this leg. Regardless of what we want, before we can do anything the horse has to start.

Isn't this obvious? Of course it is, but how many horses do you know that refuse to move when faced with a trailer ramp? Or the much-loved pony with his head down eating the grass verge that we can't get to move an inch?

Many problems are based on this absence of movement, or rather that people try, out of a desire for control, to prevent or limit movement. A horse is forced to stand still under his rider – and rears. Another horse is simply tied up and pulls back to get free. The third of our four-legged friends is put in a double bridle to try to slow him down. A horse that is standing still perhaps poses no danger, but he also can't be trained. No one needs to be afraid of a horse that is standing still, but in an emergency he will move. If horse and human haven't learnt to get on with one another, when there is movement of some form then it will just become more dangerous each time.

Many horse and rider relationships are characterised precisely by this issue. We try to switch off exactly what we actually need – our horse's movement. Once we have finally achieved this, we then take up whips and spurs to try and get the horse to move forwards again.

Rhythm and relaxed movement, the first phases of the Scales of Training, can only be achieved when we can preserve the horse's movement and steer an orderly course.

Maintaining the correct distance is one of the key elements when training your horse.

Distance

Cold water at 10 degrees centigrade does a lot of good – especially when you are soaking your swollen bruised toes in it. But somehow I had imagined my summer holidays in the Canary Islands rather differently: lying by the pool with a cold drink in my hand…

Four days previously: Five minutes into my journey on the way to a lesson I had realised that I had forgotten to bring my steel toe-capped riding boots – never mind. I was too lazy to go back and get them and the horse had been in training for some time, so where was the problem? In my thoughts I was already packing for my holiday.

The lesson ran to plan. I was standing next to my pupil chatting about my holiday. For some reason the Friesian, all 725 kilograms of him, stepped forwards, totally by chance, on to my right foot. I shoved the horse over and my foot seemed neither bruised nor particularly painful, so I forgot about it. The throbbing only really set in when I was on the plane…

I learned three things on that holiday that I don't really like to look back on:

- *Don't be lazy – when it concerns important equipment that you have forgotten, turn around and go and get it.*
- *Pay attention, no matter what's happening.*
- *Keep your distance; your toes will thank you.*

Distance, however, is far more than a matter of safety when handling horses. Many problems and resistances arise due to the fact that you don't allow your horse enough space. This in turn causes the horse's flight instinct to kick in because he no longer has the option of taking preventive measures and he feels threatened enough to take 'alternative action'. On the other hand you will quickly lose control if the distance is too great. We all know of horses that will quickly stop and turn around whilst on the lunge, thereby taking control of the situation. Knowledge of the correct distance can make the whole process of training and handling horses considerably easier.

Softness

If you have ever had a horse pull the lead rope through your hands, you will appreciate exactly how pleasant softness or compliance can be. A horse that yields softly is a pleasure – he is good to lead, lunge and to tie up, and when ridden he allows himself to be bent and flexed easily. For me this is not a far-off aim, but rather the basis of my training. This softness should be developed as quickly as possible and be maintained. At the same time, however, softness is not a question of the flexibility or gymnastic ability of the horse, but is more a mental and emotional characteristic. We can see this clearly in the fact that every horse has the capacity for enormous bend when he wants to – for example when he has an itch on his side that he needs to scratch with his teeth.

These three founding principles – movement, distance and softness – are, for me, the most important of all. There is hardly a problem

A willingness to yield can be seen especially well in halt and at the walk.

that isn't in some way, shape or form related to one of these things.

In case you consider these principles to be too simple – you're right, they are simple. They just have to be observed continuously and carefully, and followed consistently. If you want to lose weight, for example, you probably go for a run every morning and eat more healthily. It's quite simple, really.

Communication
and learning

We all have a quite specific mental picture of our horse, an idea of what he should be like and how we want to shape him. We draw this picture both consciously and unconsciously. Our four-legged partners do not differentiate between training and leisure, but rather whether a person is there – or not.

It is not only a matter of what we want to teach the horse, but also what we don't teach him or tell him. If we allow him to be pushy, he has learned that this is permissible. From the horse's point of view this becomes normal acceptable behaviour.

This flow of information is called communication. Most horses are totally confused or begin to switch off, because they are constantly receiving contradictory signals. In the grass paddock different rules apply from those in the sand paddock (arena), and the rules change daily. It is better to stay in the grass paddock, where there are clear rules. To avoid this trap we must get used to handling our horses in a consistent way and build our horse's trust in our dependability.

Communication through feeling

The majority of the time we spend with our horses is spent literally connected to them – whether through a lead rope, a lunge line or the reins. These create a constant communication, because they transmit some form of feeling. But when dealing with these tools we can get very careless – when bringing a horse out of the field you may pull the horse along behind you, but when he is being lunged he has to yield and move away. What do we actually want to tell him?

In my training programme there are only two things that I would like to communicate with a rope:

- Move – as soon as my horse and I feel something through the rope, I would like my horse to start to move.
- Direction – the pressure felt tells my horse the direction in which he has to move.

This concept is simple, and easy for the horse to grasp, as long as the handler keeps to the rules. If I am leading my horse and he feels a tug forwards through the rope this means 'Go faster' (to stop the tugging). I can 'tell' his head to yield, and thus I can turn my horse. (More on this in the section about the aids.)

Let's look now at a horse that is pulling against the lead rope. He is 'thinking' in the opposite direction. Allowing him to pull on the rope achieves the opposite of what we actually want. How many riders do you know that are, in this way, in effect telling their horses daily that it is acceptable that they want to go in the opposite direction. By comparison, if we continue to pull on the rope even though our horse is reacting correctly, we are in effect punishing correct behaviour (see page 23) and the horse will become less inclined to react in the way we would like. Everything that we do or don't do is sending a message to the horse.

For a horse, the other rider aids, such as seat and leg, are also simply a type of feeling. The horse must learn first to connect this feeling with the reaction that we are intending to create. As a result of this the horse develops an understanding of the rider's aids.

In addition to these directly transmitted feelings there are also those that are conveyed indirectly: the physical tension, emotions and willpower that the horse perceives in us. These feelings are often in conflict with the direct aids but both have somehow to be brought into harmony with each other.

It is not necessarily obvious to a horse how he is supposed to react correctly to an aid, especially if the rider stays tense, at the same time blocking the horse's movement and breathing shallowly. All of this is telling the horse that there is some form of danger – and yet he is supposed to stay relaxed and listen to the aids…

Many riders manage to confuse their horses over even the simplest of things. The majority of problems arise out a lack of, or the wrong type of, communication and the resultant teaching effect that this has. Before we start to take on the role of the 'teacher' and try to train our disrespectful and dominant horses, we need to first of all check how good our ability to communicate really is.

The learning process during training

The relationship between a horse and rider is a constant learning process. Given that this process, at least on the part of the rider, takes place primarily at an unconscious level, the resulting picture is rarely how you imagine it. How then does learning take place?

Every living creature learns, in order to improve its own condition.

If I start to get loud in a shop and am served more quickly, then this benefits me and I am likely to repeat this behaviour. If, however, I am banned from the shop, then I will think very carefully before trying it again.

Reward ensures that a behaviour will be carried out more frequently in the future. Punishment on the other hand will lead to a reduction in the exhibited behaviour. The word 'positive', when used in learning theory, doesn't mean that something is good, but rather that something is added to the process. Accordingly, 'negative' means that something is taken away.

INFO

The theme of 'learning' is clearly a more complex topic than I can do justice to here. In addition to reward and punishment, there is also negative and positive reinforcement, amongst other concepts with various definitions. It is the question of the intensity and of the timing of the stimulus that is important in training.

If we think about, for example, the leg aids it quickly becomes clear that reward and punishment are consistently connected. If the horse doesn't react or go faster, then the rider will try a whip or spurs to create the required forward impulsion. This is a positive punishment (putting on pressure). Hence 'not going forwards' is what is punished. If the horse works better, then the whip is no longer used. This is a negative reward (taking the pressure away), which will cause the horse to react to the driving aid coming from the leg. What happens though if you continue to ask with the legs? The horse is not rewarded, but continues actually to be punished for his hard work when he feels the next jab of the spurs. In this way the horse will become more and more numb, because he is being punished continuously through the never ending use of the aids. Then it is usually a case of 'He's just plain lazy'. This ignorance by riders of the horse's most basic learning behaviour is what creates one of the greatest problems for equestrian sport. Owing to the constant attention paid to the purely mechanical processes, it is possible very quickly to overlook what you are actually telling your horse when riding. The removal of pressure when the horse reacts correctly has nothing to do with any particular style or method of riding, but has everything to do with training and learning.

This system of learning doesn't, however, just work when I am trying to teach the horse something in particular. In day to day handling the same applies. It's once again down to the human partner to ensure that learned behaviour becomes a habit for herself and her horse, by sticking strictly to the rules.

What the rider
needs to know

In order to train a horse systematically, you need to have certain things always at the back of your mind.

The principle of memory cards

Only if you already have a picture in your head can you decide whether certain behaviour is desirable or not. All of us will know of the memory game in which you turn over pairs of cards repeatedly until you find two that match. This is exactly what I imagine training to be like. In my mind I turn over the first picture and wait for the horse to turn over the second card to match, or in other words to show the correct reaction to my aid.

Influencing behaviour

It is necessary to encourage the desired behaviour through reward while discouraging unwanted behaviour. Rewards can take many forms: the usual one is to release pressure from the hand and leg when the horse reacts accordingly. This does, however, mean that the horse has been put into an 'uncomfortable' position prior to this. The technique of asking the horse for less when he is working correctly and asking for more when he is not working properly follows the same principle. For example, if he is stretching down into a contact then you can let him continue, otherwise you change what you are doing and he is worked more on a

The right reaction can also consist of no reaction at all.
When touched on the hindleg Dusty neither goes faster nor becomes stressed.

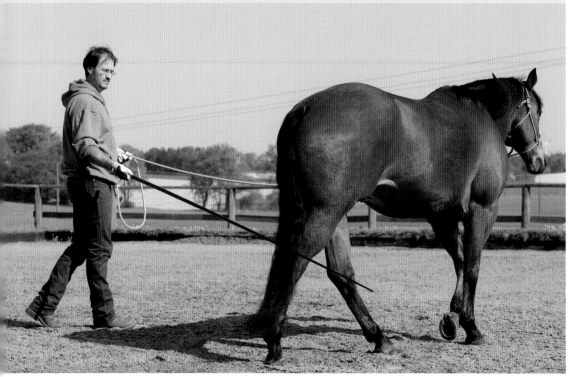

Here Dusty reacts correctly – he gives through his neck and poll and steps through with his hindleg. Now the rider's leg and hand have to stop asking. This means 'Yes, that was right' to the horse.

circle. Scratching the horse's withers and giving him a treat (preferably in connection with a clicker) are further types of reward. Do remember though that it is your horse that determines what he decides to view as a reward. If he has been standing in his stable for 23 hours then he is hardly going to see standing still as a reward.

Unwanted behaviour in the world of riding is usually punished and stopped using pain (positive punishment). To ignore bad or unwanted behaviour is possible, but not always practical. If a horse ignores your leg and is about to run into another horse, you have to take action. A good way of stopping unwanted behaviour consists of establishing an alternative reaction that makes the unwanted behaviour impossible. If your horse likes putting his head up out of your reach, then create a signal that gives the horse a reason to drop his head. For this correct behaviour the horse can then be rewarded. Punishment, on the other hand, never creates new behaviour. If your boss only

During training both horse and rider should stay calm and concentrate on the work.

ever tells you what is wrong and what you shouldn't do, you will never know what your job actually is. In an employment situation the only word for this is bullying.

When do you reward?
We always influence the last action before the praise or punishment, not the entire exercise or piece of work. On the lunge, when the horse drops his head and as a result I stop him and give him a treat, then I am rewarding the halt and the standing still, not him dropping his head!

The emotional memory

During training the horse doesn't only learn the appropriate aids, but he also memorises the emotions connected with them. If you are using a lot of whip and spurs to get the horse to move forward, thereby causing him pain, the horse will always recall these negative impressions when you use the driving aids. From this point of view, it is easy to understand why many horses have no motivation for work.

It is the intensity of the rider's aids that is decisive in terms of the horse's emotions. A rider can exert pressure with the calf, but a horse will rarely interpret this as something unpleasant. The inappropriate use of spurs, however, is seen quite differently.

Sequence of the signals

Every aid (reins, leg and seat) must initially be learnt by the horse. In doing so, though, the horse always learns the first signal. If for example you always take up the reins and then use your seat and legs to ask the horse to walk on, the horse could well learn that 'taking up the reins' means walking on. This is a peculiarity often seen in riding school horses. We must therefore teach the horse what reaction is expected from which signal, and in doing so consider how and when we give the aid.

No punishment when learning

Just imagine that you are learning something new and are punished for every mistake you make. You will very quickly give up trying to find out how to do it. When a horse does not yet recognise the aids, he will try everything possible to find a solution. As far as possible,

you should ignore the wrong answers and praise the right ones, so that the aids aren't 'poisoned' at an early stage with negative emotions. By doing it this way the horse doesn't become afraid of working with you, and by giving the horse the chance to find the right answer, you are enabling him to feel that he has control over the situation. In the end he thinks that he can determine through his own behaviour what YOU are doing. This is incredibly motivating, because every creature has the desire to be able to control a situation. This reversal of position, though, is for many riders an unbearable thought. To give an aid lightly and wait until the horse reacts correctly, even if it means that before he does he runs out for 10 metres through the shoulder, is unthinkable. When riding a dressage test this would be absolutely unimaginable; when training, though, it is exceedingly helpful. It becomes especially difficult when you are working in a shared arena and being told constantly by others that you are supposed to be giving way to them, even though it would be just as easy for them to give way to you. There is a good phrase for this type of training: **set it up and wait**...

Be clear

The more clearly you are able to transmit the picture that you have in your head to your horse, the faster your horse will learn. Divide a movement into small steps and your horse will learn it more easily. Every rein back begins with the transfer of weight backwards. These small learning steps will also help you to formulate any question for your horse as simply as possible. You should always take the time to think about the situation from the horse's point of view. If a horse has only associated your leg with 'forwards', what sense does it make

Aids are signals that the horse must learn the meaning of. Dusty has learnt that the signal from the inside (here the right) rein is asking him to move over through the shoulder.

during the early phases of the learning process to try and use it as the signal for 'backwards'? In order to teach a horse something simply you sometimes need to take detours, in order later to achieve the finesse in the reaction to the aids that will be your long-term goal. Uncomplicated thinking and good preparation will help you to ensure that your aids stay 'light'. The individual aids should be trained one by one if at all possible, and each of the exercises should be divided up into small steps.

From training to riding

For me riding begins at the moment when you ask for something that has been learnt. We all know what it's like. After a few minutes, when we have been practising the halt, it all goes exactly as we have imagined it would. But the next day it starts out noticeably worse. The reason is simple. When practising the halt we have concentrated specifically on that movement, on giving the exact aids, and then corrected or praised the horse as appropriate. During the rest of the session we have also stopped, probably when we have been doing other things like taking off a jacket. We didn't think about this halt though and it probably wasn't done correctly. When we stop twenty times without thinking about it and only ten times correctly, the horse will not improve. Learned actions must always be done correctly, when warming up, when combined with other exercises and when finishing up at the end of a lesson. The absence of consistency will always come back to haunt us. Every time you move off it should be a conscious process, just like every turn, every transition or halt. Only then do horse and rider develop experience and get into a routine. When riding, it is acceptable to give your aids more clearly or strongly on occasion – but only

when you have given them correctly up to that point and the horse knows the aid but hasn't reacted to it appropriately.

My experience is this: if you have taught the horse well and have been truly consistent with your aids, then you should nearly always be able to remain soft. Hardness is usually a result of inconsistency.

The aids

Different styles of riding have proven that you can ride horses using very different aids. The horse is not born with an understanding of what the aids mean. It is down to us to teach them. For this reason I am intending to give you no specific guidance on the individual aids – you can, for example, ask for canter in the way that you have learnt to. I am going to describe here the way that I use the aids, but in doing so I am concerned mostly with the foundations for their use.

Reins

The reins (through the hand) in general have two points at which they work: the bridge of the nose or the mouth, and the shoulder. If you take up the reins, the horse should give softly; he should give to the side through the neck and poll and show some flexion. I have never found a well ridden horse that acted differently. In addition you should be able to control the horse's shoulders through the reins. It is irrelevant whether this is actively, through the outside rein when turning, or through the inside rein that prevents the horse from falling in. The reins control the horse's head, poll, neck and shoulder.

Seat

The seat controls the speed. If I am sitting in the centre then my horse should maintain the

The seat conveys the rider's emotions. If a horse is asked to stand quietly the rider must also be relaxed and sit quietly.

pace he is at; if I sit deeper into the saddle then he should slow down, go down a pace or rein back. It is simply a question of the intensity of the aid given. Otherwise I simply try to sit as quietly as possible. Moving too much in the saddle – for example an exaggerated back and forth action with the seat or similar movements – confuses horses rather than achieving anything.

Legs

If one of my legs gives a constant pressure then the horse should move sideways and away from the pressure. If I move my leg back, then his quarters move across. If my leg goes briefly behind the girth then the horse should move his whole body sideways (as in leg yielding).

If I use both legs behind the girth momentarily, then this should increase the speed or lead to a change of pace. As an additional aid I might vibrate my legs on the girth, which may increase to a tap. In this case the horse needs to 'think' in the correct direction. A vibration with the inside leg asks for a bend to the appropriate side; vibrating with both legs causes the horse to flex more or to stretch down into the contact. These aids are useful when working towards riding with one hand in Western riding.

Weight aids

Using the rider's weight to the side (as for example when you put your weight down through the stirrup) is a very useful aid. If you use this too early, though, it may give the horse a tendency to run out through the shoulder in the new direction and possibly fall on to the forehand. I use these sideways weight aids only for steering the horse, when he has learnt to turn through his shoulder freely. This is not relevant for the exercises in this book.

I use these weight aids only in a few exercises and then as a correction. Even then I use them at a low intensity – for example to the degree that would occur when I turn my head.

The interaction of the aids

There are only a few simple aids. When you combine them, however, you can achieve everything you would wish. It is down to you, therefore, which aids take first place. I like riding my own horse from the leg and seat. The horse must still, though, react correctly to the reins, because the reins can be needed for correction in an emergency. In addition the reins are the one constant aid applied both on the ground and in the saddle, and are therefore the basis from which the other aids are established.

Riding with a counter-bend is one of the few exceptions when I would use my weight aids with a sideways action, in order to support the horse.

Processing stimuli

Over thousands of years the horse's senses have developed to meet the demands of its surroundings. As animals of flight, horses have at their disposal an ability to detect and perceive things that we can barely imagine. All of their senses are designed to detect any danger as early as possible and then to react accordingly. By using them for riding, and by the way in which we keep them today, we demand things of our horses that make their sharp senses more of a disadvantage for them. As a result horses often experience long-term stress.

It is important that all horse owners are aware of the 'other world' in which their horses live, so that they have a better understanding of what may be seen as apparently strange behaviour. Furthermore it is important to prepare the horse for life among humans by the use of targeted training.

Dealing with stimuli

In my opinion there are only three ways in which a horse deals with a stimulus, regardless of whether it is a visual, acoustic or tactile stimulus.

1. Strong stimuli usually cause a fight or flight reaction from a horse (refer to the section on distance). All of us have experienced the plastic bag in the hedge from which a horse will try to run away. This flight instinct is life preserving for the horse as a prey animal, but less pleasant for the rider.

2. When the stimulus threshold is at a level that does not set off the flight reflex, then we refer to it as habituation – in other words the horse has got used to it. This means, however, that there is a total lack of reaction from the horse to a stimulus. If your horse runs away from a specific object again and again, then it may well be that your horse becomes happier by running away and never gets used to the stimulus sufficiently to stay still. The flight instinct remains present even when your horse gets used to the stimulus – the stimulus only needs to increase and the horse will run away again. In principle nothing has really changed.

3. The way of processing stimuli that I believe to be most worth striving for is the so-called 'conditioning' process. Using this method a horse is trained to react to a stimulus in a particular way. This learning process forms a new behavioural pattern that can mask the flight instinct.

   In order to produce a good riding horse, it is important to teach them to respond correctly to the aids as well as to external stimuli. Too theoretical?

Let's take the example of a leg that is asking for sideways movement.

If the horse does not react to this stimulus, then in the horse world you would say that he is dead to the leg. A horse that runs away from the leg, though, is equally not ideal for a rider, although you would probably be surprised how many horses, including some that are competing at the highest levels, do run away from the leg. In this case, though, they are referred to as 'forward going'.

In the ideal case the horse will react by moving across to the side – a reaction with no association with flight, because a horse will almost always run away forwards as long as the way isn't blocked (for example by the rider pulling on the reins).

With regard to keeping the horse relaxed, special importance should be attached to the horse's sense of sight and to the question of how he reacts to visual stimuli.

Horses have a forward field of vision, in which both eyes receive the same information. To the sides, the field of vision means that the horse can see things with only one eye at a time. Only about 10% of a picture that is taken in with the left eye is available to the right eye. If the horse sees the same object with the right eye it is seen as something new that may be a possible danger (especially because the object is seen with a different background).

When faced with unknown stimuli a horse often shows the defensive behaviour of trying to look at the object with both eyes. A stimulus to the field of vision of the right eye tends to result more in this type of behaviour than a stimulus on the left.

This difference is not a problem in the wild because the horse can always turn its head so that the potential danger can be viewed and

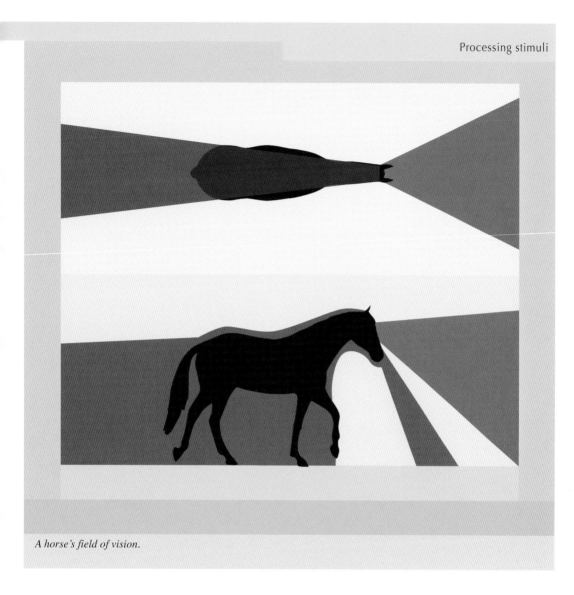

A horse's field of vision.

examined with both eyes. It gets more problematic though when the horse is being ridden on a contact or with side reins, as he doesn't have the ability to turn his head. He will then try to get some distance between himself and the object, take off or shy to the side. The contact will be lost when the horse uses his strength to ensure that he can use the right eye.

This behaviour, which is often seen by us as being more than a little uncooperative, has enabled the horse to survive and is programmed genetically. We have all probably seen horses that try to change from the right to the left rein constantly. It is not only important to train each of the eyes individually, but special attention should be paid to training a horse to 'switch' eyes.

Every horse has blind spots in which he can't see a thing. These are located behind him, directly above and underneath him, as well as directly in front of him (refer to the red fields in the picture of the horse's field of vision). 'Switching' eyes means that an object (or a person) moves from being seen by one eye, into the blind spot, and then reappears in the other eye. This sudden reappearance of a stimulus can cause the horse to try and take flight, or at least to try and turn around so that he can see the object with both eyes. If a horse is limited in his ability to run away, however, he may resort to trying to fight instead and this can cause a dangerous situation.

Stimuli can take many forms, for example a person that walks past a horse that is tied up and so moves from one side of the horse's field of vision to the other. Or even the rider's leg that swings over the horse's back and suddenly appears to the horse in his right eye.

Stress and its consequences

It is not purely from an ethical point of view that we are obliged as animal keepers to cause as little stress as possible to our horses. Stress has an unavoidable influence on the metabolism and the central nervous system of the horse, and as a result on his balance and his ability to move, both of which we require if the horse is going to reach high levels of performance. Muscle performance and growth are also dependent on these factors, because a muscle can only work correctly and grow when its state is alternating between relaxation and tension. Muscles that are under constant strain can't develop and can actually atrophy. Excitement or over-agitation is thus one of the most neglected themes in horse training. Especially in performance sport, any slight improvement in a horse's ability to resist stress can give a competitive advantage.

Stress
prevents learning and provokes reaction instead of action

Stress
activates the sympathetic nervous system

Stress
restricts muscle growth

Stress
worsens a horse's coordination and balance

You can probably best summarise this as: A stressed horse will not accept training. Think about this the next time you see a rider who is proud that she has forced a horse that is being 'difficult' and shown him who's boss.

The stress tank

Imagine that every horse has a 'stress tank' in his head that can be filled up with different events or incidents. If it overflows then we've got a mess. It is rarely one single situation that makes a horse lose its head – before the tank overflows quite a few things need to happen, although these may not appear to be too obvious at the time. At the bottom of the tank there is a small valve, through which stress can be let out – in some horses this valve is very small, in others it's very large. The aim of training is that less stress goes into the tank than flows out.

In the first steps it is a matter of starting with as empty a tank as possible, and even this can sometimes be a challenge. Often the tank is already filled, because you have taken the horse away from the rest of his herd, from the environment that he is accustomed to and that he views as safe. The stress levels are raised again when you get on and start to ride. The increased speed in trot is an additional drop to be added to the tank and canter, the speed at which a horse would normally take flight, can take the tank up to capacity. The cyclist, the lawnmower or the truck could be the infamous last straw. Is there any point in practising in the presence of any of these 'straws'?

Let's pay attention to the basics that we discussed earlier. If we strictly follow the rules that we have set when handling our horses, then the horse will be able to predict what you are going to do. The stress tank will therefore stay empty. Furthermore, your horse should never be upset by your aids. If he gets tense as a result of your aids, then you are creating exactly the stress that you are trying to avoid. You do, however, need to be able to use the aids if you want to control your horse in a situation that excites or upsets him. If your horse gets stressed, then you are to all intents and purposes trying to put the fire out with petrol. In an ideal situation your horse should react to your aids by becoming soft and accepting the aids. Training that leads towards calmness begins with the daily routine. An exercise should always be seen as only an additional means to help the process and not an end in itself.

Body control

Wouldn't it be great if you could just tell a horse to relax? This is possible, albeit somewhat differently from what you would probably imagine. Many riders try to calm their horse when he gets excited or upset, and therein lies the problem. A quiet voice or a pat is a reward but you are giving this reward at the very moment when the horse is getting upset. In doing this, although we are not encouraging the horse's fear, we aren't stopping his behaviour either.

It is possible that you will argue that you have yourself seen how a horse has calmed down when you have spoken to him quietly or stroked him. You are right, except that it worked for quite a different reason. Through the process of speaking to the horse or stroking him you have calmed down yourself and this has carried over to the horse. At this point I would like to describe how I deal with situations like this.

In the nervous system of all mammals there are two opposing nerve networks that have a mutual influence: the sympathetic nervous system and the parasympathetic nervous system.

The sympathetic nervous system serves to activate the body – if this system becomes active, the heart rate will increase, arteries will narrow, the pupils will dilate and more sweat will be produced. Digestion will slow down and the horse will get rid of any droppings he has in his system. Is this picture familiar to you?

That's right, the horse begins to get excited and is preparing himself for either flight or fight. However, the sympathetic system can also be activated in the case of physical exertion, and this is one reason why horses sometimes get too tense and normal movement turns into 'flight'.

Increased pressure towards the quarters causes Lilly to react correctly.
She turns towards me and steps round with her haunches.

The parasympathetic system, in contrast, serves to save energy and encourage recuperation; the system will be turned on to pause or rest and the processes above are reversed.

However, just as these opposing systems have an effect on the body, the body is also able to influence which of them wins out. Equine sports therapists use these systems to advantage and are able to influence the nervous system via the horse's body. You have possibly already seen how a horse can be calmed by exerting pressure on specific acupressure points.

It is also possible to calm a horse down by using certain movements. A horse in flight tends to run in a straight line, using his hindquarters strongly, holding his head up high and is generally tense all over. But what happens later when he calms down? He 'disengages' the hindquarters and turns around to face the danger. Finally he will lower his head to eat.

Through the lowering of the head, and especially the movement of the hips, the horse seems to become calmer; this is something that I experience again and again. But there is no point in trying to tie a horse's head down – the horse has to hold it low himself.

The foundation module has been devised so that the horse can be actively brought into a state of calmness, with great value being placed on working with the horse's hips.

If a horse holds his neck lower than his withers, then he will become quieter.
This only works when the neck isn't forced down mechanically using gadgets.

Distance

I was holding a beautiful black Trakehner for what was supposed to be only a short demonstration at a course I was taking. The aim was 'simply' to keep the horse at a specified distance.

After five minutes I could see my time schedule for the course disappearing into the distance and the audience was starting to get restless. All attempts to keep some space between me and the horse were answered with a strong and consistent pushing back. What worried me most though was the fact that it got worse from minute to minute, not better. From the audience I could already hears snippets of conversation along the lines of : '... dominant... assert himself... show him how it should be done...'

Something was going totally wrong here, because the horse was not exhibiting the usual sense of purpose in his actions that truly dominant horses tend to show. He looked, more than anything else, helpless. I stopped and asked the audience what they thought of the situation. The opinion was unanimous: I needed to show more dominance towards the horse.

Whether it was stubbornness or intuition on my part, I just replied, 'He is scared, he feels provoked.' In case you now think that as a result the people were convinced... I felt more like the object of their ridicule and they were probably asking themselves why exactly they had ended up here.

After this short break I began again and gave the horse a bit more rope. The horse's head came down, he relaxed and he kept the required distance with no trouble at all. After three minutes I could move him where I wanted him, even working laterally from the hand. This was a result that even I would never have expected and that had a lasting impression on me.

Knowing what the 'correct' distance is has a direct influence on the stress levels and the controllability of your horse. Alongside this, however, you have to be able to differentiate between the distances that horses select amongst each other, and the distance that horses choose to take when faced with strange objects or potential dangers.

Personal space

Within a herd a horse will maintain its own personal space in relation to the other horses, this being rarely less than 1.5 metres. When faced with higher ranking horses the distance will only ever be shortened with the direct permission of a higher ranking horse. As a flight animal the horse requires a certain distance to allow freedom of movement. If horses stood too close together the all-round view would be severely limited and could invite danger. This personal space is only impinged upon in exceptional circumstances – during social contact, adverse weather conditions or dangerous situations where flight isn't possible.

Evasive distance

Horses try to draw back to a certain distance when they feel uncomfortable about something. This distance will depend on experience, the situation they are faced with and the age of the horse, but will normally be between 1.5 and 3 metres. This evasive distance is also used when the horse approaches an unknown object. At this distance the horse will frequently circle the object in order to look at it from all sides and to assure himself that there is no danger.

Critical distance

Every horse also has a critical distance. When flight isn't possible for any reason, a horse will try to defend himself if this distance is

A sensitive horse tends to get scared when the distance between him and his handler becomes too small. The distance shown here gives the horse enough freedom, without the handler losing control of the situation.

breached. This distance is usually shorter than the evasive distance.

The meaning of distance for training

The choice of the wrong distance is the cause of the majority of the problems that occur with ground work. Many try to work their horse using a short rope, in order to control him better and to be able to stop his movement. By doing this, though, they will find themselves almost always on the edge of the critical distance. As soon as the situation gets uncomfortable for the horse (this might be due to an unfamiliar exercise, especially when working with different obstacles) he will try to withdraw and pull on the rope or, if this doesn't work, begin to get pushy and in extreme cases bite and kick.

Giving horses a certain distance when training does make them more comfortable. When starting out, you should allow the horse to retreat to his evasive distance. Keeping this distance will guarantee the horse's personal space, and the horse's vision will be less limited. This not only helps with sensitive horses, but also with dominant horses, who may feel secure but may want to cement their position by moving their handler rather than moving themselves.

Furthermore, this intermediate distance allows for the optimal control over the horse. Too small a distance will often lead to a strong reaction from the horse: pulling away, rearing, kicking, running around in a circle, or in a milder form just being bad tempered to work with, or making threats and other expressions of annoyance. However, too great a distance will mean that the horse doesn't accept the aids at all. Everyone has probably experienced a horse that won't slow down on a lunge but just continues round and round. If this occurs often enough then it will become a bad habit that will be difficult to break. Only when a horse works in a relaxed and willing manner at this intermediate distance should the distance be altered.

At greater distances the horse shows his attitude to work and whether he accepts and understands the aids. On the other hand you must be able to reduce this distance without difficulty – the training of a riding horse automatically demands that he accepts the greater restriction associated with less distance and doesn't react strongly against this. This transition must be developed gradually.

In the case of a horse that is used to normal interaction with people a distance of between 1.5 and 3 metres is a good point to start at. Only when certain prerequisites are met should this distance be altered. Even during the individual exercises it may be necessary to make this distance either greater or smaller. By doing this you will avoid confrontation, loss of control and an increase of the horse's stress levels.

The zones: white, grey and black

Let me try and put it simply: if for example your horse has just pulled free while you were trying to load him on to a trailer and all you can see is his rear end, then you are in the black zone. This means, to me, that I am working in an area in which I have no control over my horse.

In the white zone, I am perhaps 20 metres away from the trailer and everything is still fine. My horse is easy to lead and is relaxed. We both feel happy in this zone.

The grey zone can be recognised when your horse perhaps starts to get slightly nervous and is prepared to go rather hesitantly towards the trailer. He is still reacting to your aids (albeit not as well as before) and you are still in control.

This differentiation is one of the most important things, in my opinion, in training – technically you are doing everything correctly and yet despite this it still doesn't work!

In the white zone everything is OK and we are in the comfort zone. This is also the reason why we are so reluctant to move out of this zone and leave our safe area. We hate it, when we go shopping, if they have suddenly moved the goods around in the supermarket so things aren't in the aisles that they used to be. The white zone is a very nice place to be, although we know that somewhere out there a black hole lies in wait. We know exactly where our boundaries lie, and in order to avoid getting into trouble and losing control we avoid moving out of this zone. We may get unsure and transmit this to our horse. All of our efforts are aimed at avoiding stress, and in doing so we become less inclined to move.

Our horses, however, do like going out for a change and we can't always keep them under control. Afterwards we fall back into our

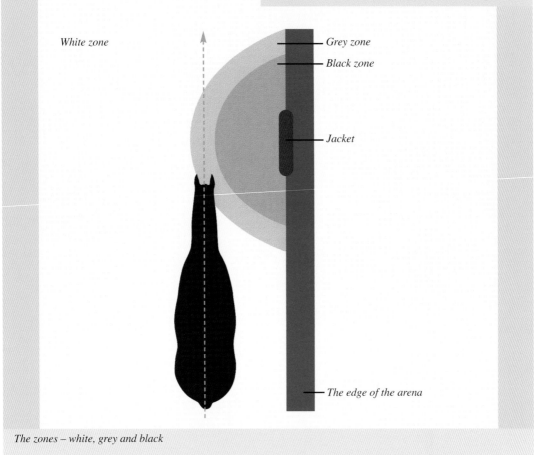

White zone

Grey zone

Black zone

Jacket

The edge of the arena

The zones – white, grey and black

comfort zone in the knowledge that in the future we will be more careful not to step over the line.

There are people that appear never to be afraid. Personally I am terrified of such people because they endanger themselves, their horses and everyone around them. It is important to recognise boundaries and to avoid venturing into the black zone. There my horse will learn that I have no control and every time I will get more afraid when I am faced with a similar situation again.

In the white zone I will make no progress (my horse won't learn to go on to the trailer if I don't try); in the black zone my horse learns that I have no control, that he can resist me (for

whatever reason) – and he still won't walk on to the trailer.

The grey zone, however, is where learning takes place. I learn that I can still control my slightly excited horse and this gives me courage. My horse learns that in spite of the tense situation he is still being controlled and nothing is going to happen to him. The art is in finding this zone and making progress while you are in it.

Unfortunately though, humankind has perfected the ability of jumping completely over the grey and landing directly in the black zone. All it needs is for someone to say the magic words 'Tell him what to do!' Or 'Don't let

The pressure placed towards his hips brings the horse into the grey zone. He is a bit tense but is still reacting correctly.

him have his own way!' When it comes to loading it becomes clearer. As you approach the trailer everything is all right. As soon as you reach a specific point though (refer to the section on distance) the horse starts to get more hesitant. Instead of stopping at this point and checking that the horse will still respond to your aids, most people will keep on going and ignore the warning signals until it's too late and the horse simply stops. And so they go back and forth for hours with the horse learning nothing at all. The oft heard comment 'Don't give up, the horse will win unless you make him go on!' has caused untold damage.

Training takes place in the grey zone and you are the only one who should determine whether you work in light grey or dark grey, depending on your ability and the time you have available. Especially when you are training by yourself, and perhaps referring to a book like this, it is crucial that you don't edge into the black zone because there is no one there to help you get out of such a situation. Should you keep ending up in the black zone you will need to find a good trainer to help you.

Taking off the pressure (retreating) when your horse reacts in the right way will cause the horse to relax, leading him into the white zone.

Advance and retreat

Here's another of these cryptic terms from the school of 'natural horsemanship' – isn't it good that I don't have to explain this one? Why? I hear you ask. You have already read everything about this particular 'secret of good horsemanship' in this chapter. You take the 'stress tank' into consideration and ensure that it doesn't overflow by stepping back, giving your horse a break or putting a greater distance between you and your horse. You might work at a 2-metre distance from the trailer and increase this to 4 metres to give your horse a break. In doing this you are moving from the grey to the white zone.

Perhaps your horse won't let you touch his ears. You should then start on his back (white zone) and try to find the place where the horse starts to show his first signs of resistance (grey zone). Leave your hands there for a few seconds then return them to his back. At the start his ears are the black zone.

The working environment

During training your surroundings are a further important factor. It starts with where the training takes place: have you got an indoor school or an enclosed arena at your disposal? Is the surface firm or slippery? Can the horse be trained in the surroundings that are available?

Trying to train a young horse in winter without an indoor school or a fenced arena is virtually impossible. There are exceptions, however, that show it is possible to train your horse by training only in the field or when hacking out. The basic rules always stay the same. However, the better the facilities, the better the results are likely to be. It is also important to consider any health issues. What use is cheap livery when your horse pulls a tendon because the surface in the school is too deep? Everyone will always try to make the best of a situation – but in poor conditions even that isn't good enough. You

A good surface and safe fencing are an advantage when training horses of any age.

should always consider carefully what you expect from your horse and whether it is possible to achieve this given the facilities you have.

Environmental factors

We can, however, be more selective when dealing with other factors. Should I try and work with my horse in a strong wind or when there is a lot going on in the yard, or would it be better not to try? As long as the horse is under control (refer to the section on white, grey and black zones), you shouldn't let yourself be influenced too much by these external factors. It is only too easy to use avoidance tactics just because there is always something not quite right. Both horse and handler require some routine in their training and this will only occur if you practise regularly. Try to find the perfect moment to work and you will make no progress whatsoever. Naturally it makes sense to ask yourself if working with your horse is really the best thing to do after you have had a hard day at work. How often, though, do you get home feeling stressed? If you want to make gradual progress you should keep to your training plan and concentrate on what you want to achieve. Having a training plan can help you really enjoy your training and forget your everyday stresses.

Designing exercises

It is particularly good for the training process if you are able to set up a working environment in which your horse can learn more easily. I always make the comparison with a children's adventure playground where children learn coordination and balance and their muscles get stronger. There your role is to keep an eye on them to ensure that nothing happens to them. Apart from that you let them get on with having fun.

In a similar way you can structure an area for your horse that allows him to develop his own abilities. With young horses in particular this is a good alternative because they don't yet work well off the aids. I will discuss this in more depth in the module on balance and coordination.

However, the training itself must be designed appropriately. You shouldn't feel as if you have to squeeze every last drop of effort out of your horse. It is possible to put the horse in a situation in which he has to find the solution for himself. As a rider your job is to steer the horse but to let him do the work. For me it is always exciting to see how horses quickly learn things independently that it takes them so much longer to grasp when the rider wants to lead them through it step

Cones help to show horse and rider the route. The horse has an optical guide and it is easier for the rider to notice when he is going off course.

by step. No show jumper actually teaches her horse to jump a 4-foot oxer – the horse learns to jump it all by himself.

In practice:
The basic principles of Gentle Horse Training

Even though all of the modules in my programme are linked, it makes sense to keep to a certain sequence. Normally I would start a horse off in the foundation module and then move on to the calmness module. With young or nervous horses I would divide these modules into ground and ridden work, starting first of all in-hand and then move on to riding. Only when the horse is responding to all the aids and is warmed up would I move on to the shoulder module. The balance module can be used at any stage, however, and can be started after the in-hand work of the foundation and calmness modules.

Overview of the exercises

Foundation module

In-hand exercises
HE1: Developing timing and focus
HE2: Basic leading
HE3: Working with the head
HE4: Working with the bridle

Ridden work
RW1: Giving through the rein circles
RW2: Giving througt the rein and leg
RW3: Encouraging stretching down using a raised
  inner hand
RW4: Bending around the inside leg
RW5: Canter circles

Applying the exercises
A1: Figures of eight: thinking left and right
A2: Transitions and gaits
A3: Moving between straight lines and circles
A4: Slalom course
A5: Halting: transitions through the quarters
A6: Figures of eight/transitions

Calmness module

Ridden work
RW6: Lateral exercises
RW7: Work on a circle
RW8: Rein back
RW9: The clock exercise
RW10: The all-purpose exercise

Calmness exercises
CE1: Basic exercise
CE2: 'Is anyone there?'
CE3: Stimulus at halt
CE4: Stimulus when moving
CE5: Backing up
CE6: Rope exercise at halt and when moving
CE7: Flag work

Collection and shoulder module

Ridden work
RW6: Lateral exercises
RW7: Work on a circle
RW8: Rein back
RW9: The clock exercise
RW10: The all-purpose exercise

Applying the exercises
A7: Figure of eight with change of flexion
A8: Figure of eight with flexion
A9: Travers
A10: Stop sign

Balance and coordination module

Single pole work
Cone forest
Cone circle
S-cones
Working on an oval
Baroque circles
Figures of eight

The exercises are structured in such a way that the previous exercises form a warm-up for the next one. It may not be immediately obvious but try to compare training with driving in the fog. You have to have travelled along a bit before the next object or place starts to take shape. Many of the exercises from different modules are similar in character – if I don't get very far with one, or I am not totally satisfied with the results, I move on to the next and return at a later point. I would usually spend about five minutes on each of the exercises on each rein (with a brief walk phase between), before giving my horse a rest

During the exercises, you should make sure that you include sufficiently long breaks.

on a long rein (when working in-hand I let him stand). You should work your horse mainly in walk and trot, ensuring that the walk is well established. I cover the canter in each of the sections (refer to the section on the) in more detail. During every training session I work on two current exercises (one in each of walk and trot), although I go over the exercises we have already covered very briefly and where necessary refresh them.

Horses are not in the same mood every day, which is why you can't always just proceed from where you left off the day before. If I am aiming, for example, to work on an exercise concentrating on my horse's shoulders but notice that he isn't giving through the rein, then I would return to an appropriate exercise that will help me work through to this submission. Before starting the training session the horse should be accepting the aids, be concentrated on his work and be able

to maintain his pace within the gait worked in. The exception to this is, of course, if I am working specifically on any of these individual areas. If I can't get the basic work right then I wouldn't move on to the shoulder module. I always do things in the same order and in the same way: controlling the movement, concentration, softness (refer to the examples given for training in the chapter 'Frequently asked questions').

Normally I wouldn't actually start to teach the horse anything new in the warm-up phase, although he should maintain his pace and direction and stay concentrated. It is important to focus on these aspects from the start. If a horse is tense from the start and is not paying attention, then I would go straight on to the basic exercises of my foundation module so that he doesn't get into any bad habits.

Foundation module

The aim of this module is to create the firm foundation that is often unfortunately lacking in our horses: a soft acceptance of the leg, rein and seat aids, and control of direction and speed. These things are the basis on which all further training of your horse relies. The majority of these exercises have gymnastic or suppling effects. You should use the simplest of these to get used to putting the learning principles into practice. You should also read the section on 'The learning process during training' from page 19 once again. The sections on theory are the tools of your trade that you always need to have in mind when working with your horse.

Timeframe

It is impossible to say how long a horse will take to learn something. While a young horse learns very quickly, it starts to get complicated as soon as a horse has learnt to think of something as 'right' that we don't actually want him to do. In this case you may have to insist on the original and desired behaviour for some time. The estimated times given are based on my own experiences. You should take the time that is necessary, but do keep a schedule of how often you are training.

Weeks 1 and 2	• In-hand work twice a week
Weeks 3 and 4	• In-hand work once a week • Use in-hand work to warm up once a week • RW 1 and RW2 twice a week including the applied exercises
Weeks 5 and 6	• In-hand work once a week • Go over RW1 and RW2 as a warm-up once a week, and then • Move on to RW3 and RW4 including the applied exercises
Weeks 7 and 8	• Ride twice a week RW1 – RW4 including the applied exercises • Lunge twice a week in trot and canter
Weeks 9 and 10	• Ride three to four times a week RW1 – RW5 (RW1 – RW4 only in the applied exercises)
Weeks 11 and 12	• Repeat the exercises • Practise and improve

On the remaining days, when exercises are not specified, you should structure the work as you wish, and in as varied a way as possible.

In-hand work

HE1:
Developing focus and timing

Aim:
This little exercise serves primarily to help you develop your ability to communicate with your horse. Using this exercise I would like to put theory into practice. The horse should start to move as soon as pressure is exerted on either the lead rope or the lunge line.

Step 1:
Stand next to the horse and take up a contact on the lead rope (for the first sign see page 18). Wait until the horse moves: initially any sign of movement will suffice, whether it be his head, his hips or his neck (refer also the section 'Be clear' on page 23). As soon as the horse moves, take the pressure off (refer to the section on negative reward on page 19). If the horse doesn't show any sign of movement, put more pressure on, by for example swinging the lead rope or slapping your leg with your hand (positive punishment, refer to page 19). Pay attention to your timing though. The horse must learn that when he finds his comfort zone, the pressure is released.

Step 2:
After this initial phase, turn your attention to the horse's legs. Only take the pressure away once the hind or forelegs have moved. For the hindlegs move the rope back towards the horse's croup; for the forelegs move the rope to the side as if following along the line of an imaginary circle.

The tug of the rope back towards her hips causes Lilly to move away with her quarters and bend her neck around. She shows the ideal neck position in response to pressure exerted on one side.

Step 3: The mare has taken the pressure off herself by stepping forwards. When I build the pressure up, the horse should release it.

Step 3:

Take the rope up in front of the horse so that the legs move forwards instead of sideways. This is the direct transition to the second exercise.

HANDY HINT

At this stage you can start to teach your horse the voice command for going forwards. When he reacts to the rope asking him to move on, give the voice command immediately before you ask through the rope. Personally I use a click of my tongue. If your horse has already learnt to walk forwards on command, then you can use this to establish the aid through the rope. In this case take up the rope and then give the voice aid – this sequence is important.

HE2:
Basic leading

Aim and use:

Here you are developing the three most important principles: movement, distance and softness. This is the foundation exercise for all further steps and is my preferred exercise as a means of correction when something goes wrong. At this stage you should be implementing the principles of learning described earlier: When should I take up the rope and when should I let it go? Is my horse keeping at the right distance and is he easy to move around? I will return to this exercise again and again if something isn't going right with my work from the ground or if the horse starts to get nervous or inattentive. If my horse is not prepared to relax and stand next to me I will work him for a few minutes using this exercise and then offer him the chance to stand still.

Lilly is working perfectly with me here. She is moving on a loose rope and is keeping her distance. Neither the handler nor the horse is feeling any pressure.

Step 1:

Stand in the middle of an imaginary small circle and lead your horse around you. To start him walking, use a light pressure transmitted through the rope to the headcollar. The distance between you and your horse should be large enough so that your outstretched arm can't touch him. At first your horse will continue to stand still. Stay where you are, drive him on but stay calm and quiet as long as he keeps moving. Push him out of your personal space when he gets too close. I prefer to push the horse out with my hand against the base of his neck. The aim is that the horse circles you.

Step 2:

As soon as the horse is quietly circling you, change the rope over to the other hand so that you are standing in the same position as when lungeing. As long as your horse keeps his

INFO

Bending exercises to one side or the other will stretch the musculature on the outside and strengthen the muscles to the inside. While the horse bends and softens he will automatically relax what might be tensed back muscles and will begin to alternately tense and relax these muscles. This ability to ask the horse repeatedly for this bend lays the foundation stone when working towards 'Losgelassenheit' (an almost untranslatable German term, best described as 'relaxedness'), which is the second step on the Scale of Training. Only a muscle that relaxes can also tense, and it is in the state of relaxation that the muscle is best oxygenated and supplied with nutrients, thus improving overall circulation.

distance, you can begin to walk in a small circle with him and give him slightly more length of rope. To bend your horse through his neck take up the rope and create a bit of pressure towards the horse's hindquarters and wait until the horse's hindlegs cross over. At this stage turn your body towards the horse's croup. As soon as the horse completes these steps go back to the first step and send him back on the circle. Your horse may stand still, not give to the pressure or try a variety of other things. Correct it all with step 1 (walking the horse in a small circle around you). Try not to react

The tug to the inside starts the turn …

My position facing Lilly's hips supports her correct reaction. Once the horse starts to walk around me in a circle again, I must turn around to face the direction of the movement.

differently to each situation as it arises. Keep your plan at the forefront of your mind. With time, your horse's legs will cross over more fluidly and you will notice that he will begin to give his head to the inside. In order to create more forward momentum you can also choose to put pressure on where the girth will be in the future, in order to prepare your horse for responding to your leg.

HANDY HINT

It is important that you introduce the horse to moving his hips away from you through the rope, or reins, rather than with the whip. Your horse will become more active through the quarters once he has understood the sequence of 'pressure taken up through one rein – softening – crossing over' because the rein is the first signal. This will be an enormous help later when starting work on collection.

... and causes the hips to swing out.

Once the horse is standing facing me, the rope leads her nose round to the new direction ...

Step 3:

Turning, halting and reining back. For the halt you simply have to let the hindquarters swing out for longer than in step 2. As a result of the turn the inside foreleg will come to a standstill and then when you stop exerting pressure the horse should stand still. Stopping in this way will ensure that the horse stays soft through the neck and steps underneath himself. Halting with his head up high and with a tense back should be avoided, otherwise he may get used to doing it this way rather than correctly. As soon as you see that your horse stops easily, then you can exert a light pressure on his nose (with the halter) and ask for one or two steps of rein back. At the end you will be standing facing the horse's head. To turn him after halting, show him the new direction with the rope (for example to the right out of your line of sight) and lightly touch his outside (in this case the right) flank. Thus you are already training the aids with the inside rein and the outside leg. Watch out that in the turn your horse maintains his distance and moves his shoulder away. He shouldn't run out to the front or push you to the side.

... and asks her to go in the opposite direction. Here Lilly doesn't move her shoulders over enough so that she comes a bit too close to me. Try to stay where you are and bring the horse to a halt if he threatens to try and push you away.

After the turn Lilly is working correctly again on the other rein.

57

The turn has brought Lilly to a halt.
The pressure backwards has then caused her to take a step back.

As soon as you have had some practice with this exercise it is sensible to change the leading hand. Use both hands on both reins because during schooling it may often be the case that you don't have the time to swap over the rope and whip at every change of direction.

Step 4:
Straight lines
Connect small circles with straight lines. Choose a point on the outside track of your arena and go along it in a straight line. Your horse should maintain his distance and match your speed, which you should also vary. If the horse gets too close and resists being sent

further away stand still and send him on to a small circle. Do the same if he goes too fast. You should take up the usual leading position during this step – stand to the left of the horse when leading on the right rein.

HE3:
Working with the head

The horse's mental and emotional state can be easily identified by the tension shown through his head and neck. No nervous or tense horse is likely to give up the most sensitive part of his body freely. Working with his head is therefore vital when working towards a relaxed horse.

Step 1:
Begin by massaging or stroking the horse's head and neck until the horse starts to relax or at least tolerate your touch. If a horse doesn't like being touched it is unlikely that he is going to move this part of his body. Include the area around the nose and mouth but the horse must not try to nibble the handler.

Step 2:
Create light pressure with your fingertips on the side of the head turned away from you and wait until the horse – no matter how little – turns his head towards you. Think about your timing: if you remove your hand when your horse tries to lift his head then he will learn to evade you by lifting his head. After the horse has reacted in the correct way a few times, ask again as many times as necessary until he turns his head clearly towards you (i.e. he clearly bends his neck to the side) and keeps it there. Practise this on both sides.

Use the halter and the rope to create these responses. If for example you are standing to the left of the horse and holding the rope with your left hand then you can use your right hand to support the command by exerting gentle pressure at the base of his neck to encourage him to give towards you.

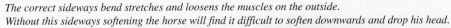

The correct sideways bend stretches and loosens the muscles on the outside.
Without this sideways softening the horse will find it difficult to soften downwards and drop his head.

Practise asking the horse to give to you through the rope and halter.
Because of the missing contact on the outside the horse's head position is acceptable.

If a horse lowers his head easily then putting his halter or bridle on will be child's play.

Step 3:

Allow the horse to move his head to the side and then place your other hand on his poll and exert gentle pressure until the horse drops his head. If he resists, move his head gently back and forth with the halter to loosen the poll. Once the horse has shown that he can drop his head when his head is bent slightly towards you, you should do the same with his head and neck straight. Don't be put off by resistance; simply go with him if he tries to back away.

HANDY HINT

Once you have tried some of these smaller exercises you will realise what often makes training so problematical. There are so many things that you have to be aware of simultaneously. First of all you actually have to know what you are trying to achieve to ensure that you can reward the horse when he does it right. You have to watch your horse carefully and reward the right attempts by immediately taking any pressure off or stopping asking. If you are working with the rope or the reins then you will also feel the responses through your hand. At the same time, however, you have to keep an eye out for any incorrect responses and react accordingly without forgetting your ultimate goal. If your horse has dropped his head, for example, but has stepped back at the same time, he will learn that backing up is a means of evasion. Add to this your and your horse's feelings, and there you have a typical training session.

HE4:
Working with the bridle

Given that the feeling transmitted through the bit will be felt differently from that given through the halter, when working in his bridle for the first time, your horse may not, necessarily correlate the two. Compared with a bitless bridle or halter, the important advantage of a bridle and bit is that you can control the lower jaw. If you are able to relax the jaw using some form of signal, the horse is more likely to relax through his neck and poll. The lower jaw is a good starting point for loosening the entire horse – if he is tense in his lower jaw he will usually be tense throughout his

entire body. However, by constantly exerting pressure through the bit you will restrict the horse's ability to learn and cause him to tense up.

Step 1:
Standing in front of your horse, who has a bridle on, take hold of the bit rings with your fingers. Take up a light contact towards his cheeks (up and back towards the corners of his mouth). You can if you wish fix your hands in the cheekpieces or hook them into the headpiece. As soon as the horse opens his mouth even slightly, stop and praise him. With older horses it could take longer before you get this reaction – just build this exercise into your daily training programme. As soon as your horse responds consistently to this you can move from holding the bit rings to holding the reins instead, but using the same pressure in the same direction. In this way you can start to establish a signal that you can also use when in the saddle to loosen the horse's jaw and ask him to stretch down and take the rein.

Step 2:
Repeat HE1 and HE2 with the horse bridled up, and give the signals in the same way. For horses that are perhaps not so soft in the mouth you might need a bit longer. Don't fall into the trap of using more force and pulling more strongly, but instead use your other hand to encourage the horse forwards, or just take more time. To avoid pulling the bit through the horse's mouth, attach the rein or rope to a chin strap connecting the bit rings and running underneath the horse's chin. These can be found in many Western outlets and are also available from saddlers. They are often used when leading youngsters in-hand to avoid putting pressure on the bit. If you can't find one specifically for the job

Sciona working on basic leading using the bridle.

you can also use a spur strap. When working young horses you should also use a halter and rope so you don't have to pull on the bit too much if the youngster decides to take off.

INFO

A horse should play with the bit in his mouth. This movement of the tongue muscles loosens the muscles in the jaw and poll. You can't move anything with your teeth clenched, after all. The muscles are connected directly to the musculature of the lower neck, so the horse will also relax. As a result of this 'sucking' of and playing with the bit the horse will lower his neck and thus stretch the neck ligaments and the ligaments that run down the length of the spine. This stretching pulls the vertebral spinous processes forward, rounding the back and allowing the legs to move more freely. If the horse sets his jaw because he feels too strong a contact this blockage will be carried on through the whole spine, which will lead to a loss of impulsion and cause shortened strides.

The chin strap will prevent the bit being pulled through the horse's mouth when taking up a contact through one rein.

Starting mounted work

The many courses that I have run over the last few years have taught me a lot. Despite the many and varied riding styles, horse and rider always seem to encounter the same problems. Only a very few horses react to the aids in such a way that they allow you to ride them into 'Losgelassenheit' (in English, loose relaxedness or suppleness). Most horses will react to both rein and leg with at least a degree of tension. But these are the essential basic aids that are required for all riding. Thus the very aids that are needed for the training process are often not available to us.

A little test

Try this test for fun. Ride on a straight line with the reins held loosely in one hand. Lift the hand carrying the reins a little higher and with the other hand take up one of the reins and take up a gentle contact. Watch your horse's reaction carefully.

Any well ridden horse that I have tried this with has reacted in the same way: they yield to the pressure and flex through the poll. They softened, in other words.

More frequently, though, you see quite different reactions. Most horses will lift their heads, tensing up and hollowing the back. Other horses will stiffen through the head and neck, tilting the head towards the contact and dropping out through the shoulder, unbalancing themselves and falling on to the forehand.

You should quite rightly notice that the other aids that would prevent these faults are missing. But what if the horse misunderstands these other aids, just as he has the aid through the rein? Perhaps the horse can be put into 'shape', but what about his relaxedness and suppleness?

These basic exercises should teach the horse the correct reactions to the aids, whether he has learnt them already or not, or even if he has learnt them incorrectly. Horses that are ridden correctly, with softness, will learn these exercises very quickly and will find them easy to do – others will learn at their own pace.

HANDY HINT

The horse's sequence of movement is fairly complicated. As soon as there is even the smallest of disruptions it has an effect on the entire movement. One of the most challenging tasks facing a rider is trying not to interrupt this sequence with the seat, legs or hands. Only when you can appear to be invisible on your horse can you really have an impact on this movement. Very few riders can sit so independently in the saddle that they don't interfere with their horse. Add to this the rider trying to exert her influence (usually at the wrong moment) and the horse's movement will be severely hindered. In the basic exercises it would actually be best to give away the reins totally and just ride with a relaxed and passive seat. Try to let yourself be carried and try to fit each of the exercises into the horse's natural movement. This isn't just important because of the way a horse learns (every disruption acts as a punishment to the horse because he will find it unpleasant); it is also a chance for you to work on your seat.

RW1:
Giving through the rein/circles

What should this exercise look like? You should be sitting comfortably on your horse and resting your inside hand on your thigh. The horse should be walking on a volte/small circle (10 – 15 metres), and giving through his neck and poll. Strictly speaking a volte is usually 10 metres but with young horses this can put strain on their joints if worked on too much. Without any further aids the horse should remain on the circle, not falling onto his inside shoulder nor drifting with his quarters to the outside (this often happens if the horse is falling onto his forehand or pulling against the contact), nor should he run through his outside shoulder (and thus try to avoid the bit).

In this exercise the horse should learn to give to the inside rein and rebalance himself. At this stage it will become clear what influence the rein has on a horse's head, neck and shoulders. This isn't a riding exercise in the usual sense. It is putting the horse into a position where he learns how to move himself. You are just giving him the means to do so, just as a child will quickly learn to ride a bike when she is given one.

Step 1:

Head and neck. Most horses will start by trying to fight against the pressure (refer to page 63). They will lift the head up or to the side, rest on the bit or try to find other evasions. Don't worry about this; just wait until the horse, even briefly, gives through his neck and head to the side and you clearly feel less pressure in your hand. At this moment you should give with the rein and continue to ride on in a relaxed way. Repeat this exercise on both reins for three to five minutes until you can start to rely on his response and he starts to react more quickly. Although you may eventually hope to feel no pressure through the rein at all, at this

Sciona is giving softly to the inside without falling in on her shoulder.

point it is too early to expect this because we haven't worked on getting the correct reaction through the shoulder.

Step 2:
Controlling the shoulder. From here the horse shouldn't just yield through his neck and poll, but should be moving his shoulder. Your horse will probably have tried to make the circle larger or smaller when working on a small circle. If he has tried to reduce the size of the circle then you need simply to use both legs to drive him forwards until he moves back on to the original circle.

If on the other hand your horse is running out through the shoulder then you will need to use your outside leg together with your outside rein in short half-halts. Do this until he stays on the circle without drifting out through his shoulder. Don't keep a hold on the outside rein but rather give and retake the rein, because if you keep a constant hold there is a danger that your horse will pull against the pressure in turn and just get stiffer.

From halt to walk:

Dusty moves out of the halt well without leaning on the reins.

Step 3:
Walking on, and the halt.
At halt, ask the horse to give to the side by holding one rein on your thigh. Should your horse try to take a step this is because he is still pulling against the rein (and is becoming unbalanced enough to need to take a step to regain his balance) or he is unbalanced. If this is the case then wait until the horse stands still again and gives to the rein. To ask the horse to walk on lift your pelvis up (as if you were going to get up out of a chair) and only then ask with your legs. At first the horse will try to get away from the one-sided pressure and will possibly start to spin or turn around. With practice though he will move off, bent in the right way and walking on a circle. Let him go round several times. Now sit deep into the saddle. Wait until your horse stops and relaxes. Then let the reins go and let him stand for a moment. At the

start the horse will probably start to try and spin around. Over time though the horse will learn to balance himself more and will actually halt on the circle. It is very important when doing this that the outside rein is kept long, otherwise this pressure will be felt by the horse and he will transfer his weight on to the inside shoulder and be unable to halt.

INFO

What lies behind this?
Thoughts on the training process

At this point I would like to clarify in technical terms what lies behind this apparently simple exercise.

Here he has slightly lost his balance and fallen on to his inside shoulder, drifting out at the same time through his quarters. The rider will feel this because it will cause him to sit to the outside.

Dusty has pulled himself back together and is in the correct position again. Walking on and halting is difficult and requires much practice.

You will have noticed already that we are trying to get the horse to respond to your seat. With regard to the process of learning, the signal that needs to be learnt should always be the first one given. In this case it is your weight that is the aid. Of course no horse will stop just from this aid initially, and you won't be able to get away from the need to use the reins to bring him to a halt. If you use both reins, however, the horse will probably lift up his head, become tense and lean on his forehand, becoming unbalanced. If we halt like this often enough it will become a habit. It won't get any better, and on the contrary will probably get worse.

Use the method detailed above to get around this problem. Very few horses will continue to walk for hours on end if you ride as described. The way you position the reins makes it practically impossible. Given that you hold the reins the same way in walk as in trot, it is your seat that gives the first signal for the halt. If you were always to take up the rein and then sit deep in the saddle the reins would be the first signal and the horse would not learn to stop from the seat and your weight. Furthermore, he has to soften and balance himself. From the start therefore the halt teaches the horse what you want when riding, regardless of whether English or Western: to listen to your seat and stay balanced and soft on the aids. As we continue the exercise can be changed so that you can halt according to the particular style you are riding in.

If the horse has improved his balance as a result of the previous steps,
then he is better able to carry himself and doesn't need the reins to support him.

Step 4

Rein variations.

As soon as your horse can do the previous exercises, and stay balanced and soft, it is time to take up a more correct position with the reins. The way you have held the reins up to now serves to help the training process. Instead of fixing the inside rein on your thigh, it is now time to take up both reins with a light contact. It is important that your hands follow the natural 'nodding' movement of the horse's head back and forth. Setting your hands would stop this natural to and fro and could lead to inactive muscles along the length of the horse's back, causing the horse to step up short with a tense or hollowed back. With a light contact and using your seat you should be able to keep the horse on the circle. If at any time he doesn't halt when asked, change back to the previous position (inside rein on the thigh and the outside rein loose). Even if your horse tries to block you totally, correct this using the position of the reins. Another variation is riding on a totally loose rein and halting by using your seat alone. The more you vary the position of the reins, the better the horse will react to your seat. Try to train using both variations and not just the one you would normally use for your style of riding. If your horse loses his outline when riding on a loose rein then take up the contact again briefly, establish the correct shape and then give with the reins again. As soon as your horse can do this in walk to your satisfaction try it in trot.

Britta and Sciona show a good contact with no sign of leaning.
Varying the way you hold the reins is important for the horse when he is learning to listen to your seat.

RW2:
Giving through the rein and leg

What should it look like?
In this exercise the leg and rein on the same side are working together. The horse should move his quarters over while giving softly to the rein. The position of the head supports the movement created by your sideways driving leg, and at the same time the leg is helping the horse to react softly to the rein because he can't set his neck when he is crossing over with his hindlegs. The aim is for the horse to respond to both aids and become soft through his body.

Your leg shouldn't cause the horse to want to run away, but instead should encourage a more active hindleg, which is shown by his legs crossing over. Furthermore the exercise has a suppling effect and the back muscles will be loosened – an important prerequisite for a loose shoulder and active hindquarters.

As well as the benefits already described, owing to the increased control over the horse's hips you get two other important side effects: control over direction and control of speed. If you move your horse's hips to the 'east' your horse will move to the 'west'. While many horses will run out through the outside rein and through their shoulder at the start of training, and determine their own direction, with the ability to control the hips you have a better chance of having some sort of influence on this. In addition, using these types of turn will

Dusty reacts softly to both hand and leg.
His inside foreleg has stopped as a result of his hips moving over.

slow the horse down. The horse learns to stay soft and there is no tug of war between horse and rider. The instinct for flight gets systematically trained out of the horse instead.

Step 1:

If your horse tries to run away from your leg or refuses to move this is an ideal exercise. Again, timing is crucial to the learning process. If I take my leg away as soon as my horse goes faster, then he will learn how to get away from pressure and will tend instead to run away more from the leg. Instead the aim should be that such horses move

their quarters over and go more slowly! Ride a circle as described in RW1. Now bend your horse to the side (refer to HE1, Step 2), so that he will be forced to move his quarters over, and put your leg on lightly behind the girth, on the same side. The inside rein should now be taken up in the direction of the withers. Keep your leg where it is and sit deep in the saddle (refer to RW1) until the horse starts to slow down. At this moment relax all the aids and let your horse step out of the circle.

Dusty has come to a halt without stiffening up through his neck or back.

INFO

Why does this make a horse slow down?

The idea behind this exercise is simple. When the quarters are moving fast enough around the forehand, the inside leg will slow down (as if, when roller skating, you held on to a lamppost and skated round in a small circle). As a result of this reduced forward movement of the inside leg the horse will slow himself down.

Step 2:

At the next stage your horse should not only step around with his hindquarters but should also soften through the rein. You just might have to wait a bit longer.

Step 3:

Keep an eye on the inside foreleg. As soon as it stops moving, take the pressure off and sit deep in the saddle. Your horse should halt. If the horse runs out, simply repeat the exercise until he is standing still. (This exercise is the same as HE2 Step 3.)

Problem solving:

1. If the horse halts but doesn't soften:
   Release all the aids, walk the horse forwards and start the exercise over again. The horse shouldn't be given a break because this sends the wrong message. Go back to the in-hand work and try to improve this (HE1, Step 2).

2. If the horse runs out through his shoulder:
   Of course you can easily contain the horse with your outside rein. Most horses, though, react by setting themselves against the rein or tensing up. For this reason I try not to use this method of correction at this stage (at least before we get to the section on the shoulder). Instead position your horse's head more to the inside and push more with your legs to create greater energy. If this doesn't work then ride a circle as described in RW1. Try doing the exercise as soon as the horse has started to walk on (within the first two steps). A slower walk often helps you more.

Sciona lets herself be sent into a long and low outline by hand signal.
This is a way of asking the horse to relax.

RW3:
Encouraging stretching stretch down using a raised inner hand

Once your horse is responding well to HE4 it is time to carry this exercise over to the saddle. Ride on a small circle and lift the inside hand so that the horse feels the bit acting gently on the inside corner of his mouth. Keep the hand raised until the horse releases his lower jaw and drops his head slightly. As soon as he does this drop your hand back to where it was. The outside rein should stay on a normal contact and although you can lift both hands up, this does tend to put the rider out of balance. When the horse responds consistently it is important to remember that the inside hand should be lowered slowly, otherwise the horse might learn this as the aid to pull his head down and lean on your hand instead.

If your horse doesn't respond correctly you can support the rein and hand aid with your inside leg (RW2).

RW4:
Bending around the inside leg

Until this stage the horse has always bent in the direction of the inside leg. We can now use this to teach him to bend (i.e. flexion) with the inside leg aid.

Ride a larger circle with a light contact through both reins (RW1 Step 4). Instead of asking more with the inside rein, start to create a light pressure through both reins. Immediately afterwards, 'rub' or 'brush' your inside leg on the girth until the horse starts to bend in this direction. As soon as he starts to bend stop rubbing and give both hands forwards (negative reward). If the horse doesn't soften let your leg move slightly backwards and push the horse's hips over until he starts to bend around the leg and flexes along his length (i.e. longitudinally – also called direct bend). This is our start: giving through both reins. This exercise can be done at both walk and trot. The stimulus created through the use of your leg should make the horse think in the appropriate direction (compare this to the section later in the module on calmness).

With this exercise your horse will not only learn to flex and bend, but it will also teach him to stretch through his length and take the contact down (as long as you are giving him the rein and are asking him to stretch down). If this doesn't happen you could try lifting your inside hand (RW3) in order to ask for this direct flexion.

Applying the exercises

The following exercises are an application of the basic exercises shown so far. Any problem solving will always use the methods already covered. You will soon see how varied and effective you can make the structure of your training sessions. It is not just about completing the exercise, but also how you complete it, ensuring that the horse stays soft through the rein, keeps his shoulders where they should be and is reacting to your seat. These things should be developed with the following exercises and will make the transition to real riding possible.

A1:
Figures of eight: thinking left and right

Change the rein as soon as your horse has successfully completed an exercise on a volte. Ride a straight line of one to two metres between voltes so that the horse can straighten before going into the new bend. He should stay supple and not fall on to the inside shoulder when changing the bend. You may find

A brush with the inside leg will bend your horse to the inside. The rider's hands must allow this to happen.

The moment of change – I let my right hand drop down to take up the rein. I won't touch the new outside (left) rein again to prevent either myself or the horse pulling on it.

fortable tempo in every pace. If he is too fast in trot then use the exercise to slow the trot or to make the transition into walk.

A3:
Moving between straight lines and circles

Start to ride more on straight lines. If your horse gets faster or you lose his outline then go back on to the circle until you get what you want. If he tries to take over by starting a circle in one direction, then ride a volte in the opposite direction. Your horse should move straight until you ask him to do something else (controlling direction). I like to use this when warming up so that I can establish control over both the direction and speed of my horse.

A4:
Slalom course

Place several cones in the arena and ride sweeping curves around them. Make sure that you are controlling your horse's hips by moving the corresponding inside leg back while at the same time taking the inside rein in the direction of the diagonally opposite outside hind. In this way the horse will able to be complete the circles while staying soft and relaxed. Pay attention to your seat, so that the horse doesn't halt during the turns. You can do this exercise in trot or walk. As you and your horse get more practised, leave your leg on the girth rather than moving it back.

that your horse will not get faster when going straight but may actually go rather more tentatively. This is quite normal, because he is waiting for the next command. He is likely already to be thinking about stopping. Use the opportunity to ask for a halt through your seat without touching the reins. If it takes more than two steps to stop, turn him to get the halt (RW1).

A2:
Transitions and gaits

Use RW1 for the trot as well as for the transitions down to halt. Your horse should move at a com-

A5:
Halting: transitions through the quarters

Start to use your ability to control the horse's hips with your seat to ask for downward transitions and halts. The fine tuning between your seat and your leg determines whether your horse stays in a particular pace or makes a downward transition.

A6:
Figures of eight/transitions

This exercise is ideal for making transitions smoother. Ride a circle in walk on the left rein and halt by asking the horse to move his hips over (RW2). Sit deep and make yourself heavy in the saddle when doing this. Once the horse is standing still, start thinking to the right, take up the right rein and ride off slightly to the right. Once you get back to the centre of the figure of eight use your right leg and the right rein to ask for the transition to halt. You have completed the exercise successfully when your horse can halt and move off well on both reins. When you are confident with your own ability to ride the exercise and coordinate the aids, try it again using trot-walk transitions. With practice you should be able to ride your horse through the transitions just by using your seat.

Canter work

The canter, which is for many riders their favourite pace, creates problems for more than a few. The reasons for this are often the same.

The seat

You can often see how riders bang into the saddle with every canter stride while at the same time either yanking on the horse's mouth or holding on too tight. Often when moving into the canter the horse jumps up into the rein and hurts himself – in effect being punished for doing what he is being asked. That horses either race around at a flat-out trot or have an extremely tense canter as a result is hardly surprising. Although it's tough, the only thing that will help is being lunged at canter on an experienced horse. Until you feel comfortable being lunged without reins at canter, you won't advance far.

INFO

In order to improve and centre the rider's seat there are lots of suitable exercises that don't involving a horse such as unicycling, balancing on tree trunks, climbing walls or similar. Especially effective is regular use of a so-called Snaix NeuroBike, because in order to steer it successfully you have use similar balance to that used when riding a horse.

The Snaix NeuroBike is steered by rotating the hips. Look where the steering joint is – in the middle! This offers the optimum type of exercise for coordination, especially for riders, and has a long-lasting effect on your seat.

In the early stages of training young horses I have nothing against short sessions of canter. Don't use too much canter at this stage.

Thoughts of flight

Unfortunately you see this scene everywhere – a young horse will be put on a lunge and chased around into canter with much cracking of the whip. When ridden he will often be allowed to fall into canter after racing round at a flat-out trot, again usually with the help of a whip or spurs. As already detailed in the section on the emotional memory, the horse remembers the feelings associated with this and will always connect the canter with thoughts of running away; it is after all the usual way that a horse

takes flight. If the horse also then gets tense as a result of the aids given by the hands and the seat, chaos is ensured. You must not use the flight instinct to chase a horse into canter. It takes a long time to change this type of behaviour once it has been learnt.

Balance

The feeling of being on a sharp incline when riding on a circle in canter has probably been experienced by every rider – it's a bit like cornering on a fast motorcycle! The reason for this is that in general horses want to support themselves more on one shoulder than the other, usually the right one. The resultant loss of balance is usually compensated for by speed at canter with an accompanying increase in stress levels. In this case work on the balance module is recommended!

If your horse doesn't possess a good (and quiet) canter, then you should do the exercises in this book first in walk and trot before moving on to the foundation exercises in canter, because the wrong sequence of movements can be memorised in canter just as easily as the correct one. Overall everything goes better and faster when the horse is well prepared.

RW5
Canter circles

Step 1:

Ride one or two circles in canter and then go into walk. Check that you can do the basic exercises with the horse remaining soft and supple and check whether he has tensed up. If he has become tense go back to the initial exercises until he can do these as well as he did before starting the canter work. You should work with your horse calmly and ensure that he can be controlled easily throughout. Go back as far as you need to. After this, walk your horse in a long and low outline for a few minutes and then start over again. In this phase of training we are concerned with recognising how nervous your horse becomes during canter and then reducing this level of nervousness. The exercises involving moving the horse's quarters over are particularly good for this.

Step 2:

Move into canter again on the circle and ask your horse to bend through the inside rein. Sit deep into the saddle until he makes the transition down to walk. Try to keep him at a moderate speed, and bend the horse in if he does get too fast. Finish by riding a few 10 metre circles in trot or walk to encourage suppleness.

Step 3:

Change the pace through walk, trot and canter, ensuring that the downward transitions are always ridden through the seat and inside rein.

Step 4:

Ride figures of eight in canter using the bend to achieve simple changes. This equates to the exercise A6, although the transition isn't yet achieved by using movement through the quarters.

REMEMBER

Downward transitions from canter

In order to achieve a successful downward transition from canter using bend to the inside, you will need to watch out for several things. Your horse should respond to the aids well in both walk and trot, at the same time staying soft (refer to RW1). He should not get too fast and you need to be working on a good surface. Wet grass is not generally suitable for schooling but is especially unsuitable for this particular exercise.

Calmness module

If you would like a calm and relaxed horse, many factors will play a role. Good sense, composure and calmness are as much due to character as to the way a horse is kept. Despite this it is amazing how successful appropriate training can be. A horse that is calm is not just a pleasure for his handler or rider. This calmness is also good for the horse himself.

Even when, in this chapter, I am dealing specifically with calmness and composure, the horse's state of health will have a significant impact on the entire training programme and how we handle him. To a certain extent these factors must also be considered if you are going to continue to work through any training programme successfully. Being ridden isn't a natural state for any animal of flight and even after years of riding many horses still experience some underlying stress. The aim of this entire module is to reduce this stress. Part of this is that the horse needs to stop thinking about running away. Pressure (no matter what the source or cause) shouldn't result in flight but rather make the horse 'think' towards people. All the exercises are aimed at making the horse react to pressure in a way different from that his nature demands.

When working through this module you will find that some horses become very sluggish – the very opposite of forward going. This is totally normal because they are no longer feeling threatened and that they have to run away. Horses such as these have never learnt to be driven on because in their minds they were always 'on the run'. In this case the signal to go forwards has yet to be established. For this reason never start this module until the basic exercises are well established in-hand. You need to have control of a horse's hindquarters, especially in the case of sensitive horses, for reasons of safety.

If you are working with laid back and slower horses, it can happen that they become even slower and just want to remain standing by you (we are after all trying to teach them that the solution to every problem lies with their handler). With this type of horse it is absolutely essential that they move on when asked and keep the correct distance.

The rider as a source of stimulus

In an emergency, horses react to a stimulus either with flight or with a safety response in which they turn towards the danger and try to assess it with both eyes. A rider and equipment, from the saddle to the whip, act not only as a stimulus, but they occur in the horse's blind spot (above the horse) or far enough to the side that a horse's normal reactions aren't possible. He can't get himself to safety, and running away will only work if he manages to buck the rider off. This constant bombardment with stimulus in such a vulnerable place can result in long-term stress for some horses. This has a lot to do with bad habits such as not standing still when a rider tries to saddle up or to mount. Add to this a horse getting tense as a result of the aids and his central nervous system switches on to alarm (refer to the interaction of the sympathetic and parasympathetic nervous systems) and suddenly every stimulus out of the horse's sight becomes a source of danger.

External stimuli

External stimuli can of course also cause stress but they are rarely sufficient alone to cause the horse's stress tank to overflow. Often the situation escalates in other ways. Something external might distract the horse's concentration from his rider – every rider has at some stage found her horse suddenly becoming spooky. At this moment the horse is no longer on the aids and the rider tries to exert her will to get the horse's attention back on the job at hand. A horse may not be able to cope with this increased pressure from the rider to concentrate and the situation goes from bad to worse. Many riders avoid this happening by leaving the horse alone to get over the fright, or intentionally showing their horse something that might be perceived as dangerous. This can work well but for many reasons isn't necessarily ideal.

On the one hand you can't let your horse investigate the judge during a dressage test to show him that she isn't so bad after all, and on the other you are thus allowing your horse to decide whether an object is dangerous or not. If I ask my horse to approach something he may suddenly decide that it's dangerous, do a 180-degree turn and take off in the other direction. You have given control of the situation away. In the first module we have laid down the foundation. The horse should respond to our aids by softening and our control over him has improved. In the following exercises we go a step further.

Practical exercises to improve concentation

The most important prerequisite for a calm horse is his concentration on his handler or rider. Without this the horse will be continuously searching his surroundings for dangers and independently reaching his own decisions. It's not that a horse shouldn't look around any more, but rather that he shouldn't be looking around to check everything is safe. Instead he needs to accept that he must concentrate on his human.

CE1:
Basic exercise

This exercise serves not only to improve concentration, but also it is my 'emergency' exercise that I always fall back on if the horse tries to take flight. It has been developed out of the in-hand exercise HE2. The aim is that your horse should first go around you on a 10-metre circle but then move his quarters out. As a result of this movement the horse comes to a halt in front of you with both eyes turned towards you. In the initial exercises we achieved this by putting

pressure through the halter on to his head. This should now happen with more pressure placed towards his quarters.

Step 1:
Start the horse off on a small circle. As in the basic exercise take up a soft contact on the lead rope and slap your other hand on your thigh. At the same time turn towards the horse's hip. The aim is to cause the horse to move his quarters over as a result of placing more pressure on him (the noise and your movement) and thus to get him to stand. If the horse stops moving then you have to increase the pressure. However, if he starts to try and run away keep up the pressure but use the lead rope to cause his quarters to swing out. As soon as the horse has halted and is looking at you take all the pressure off him and stand still as well.

Step 2:
As soon as the horse looks away from you, for example from your perspective he looks away to the right, then you walk to the left towards his hip. As soon as the horse looks at you again, stop. It doesn't matter whether he has to move his quarters to do this or whether he just straightens his head up. Strictly speaking the horse thinks he is controlling you: 'As long as I am looking at that idiot, she won't do anything stupid.'

Step 3:
Walk towards the horse's hip again; when he turns towards you he is 'thinking' towards you, by giving you his attention. If he is thinking away from you, he will move forwards on the circle. As soon as he is following you with his neck, you can start to go in small circles around the horse. The horse will not only turn with you, but his forelegs should also be moving and follow you around. As the horse starts to

1

Step 3: Walk towards the horse's hip.
He will turn towards you because he is giving with his quarters.

Finish off the circle – the horse should start to walk next to you.

3

2

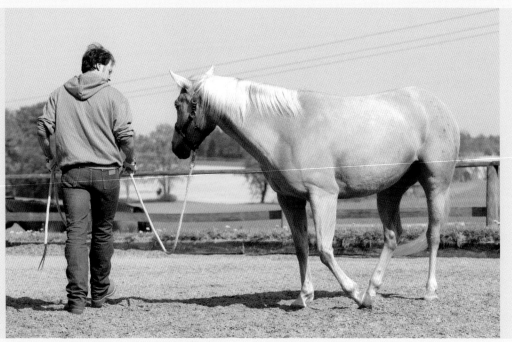

Don't approach his hips anymore, but instead follow the line of his hindquarters.
Now the horse's forelegs should also start to move.

Allow the horse to follow you. If he stops moving go round in a half circle towards his hip again.

4

1

Step 4: Practise putting pressure towards his hips so that the horse turns towards you.

2

Take the pressure away …
… and start to walk backwards. Try to make yourself smaller when doing this.

3

follow you, you can turn this into leading practice, without needing the lead rope. In step 2 I am teaching my horse to stand still without me having to hold on to him.

So what is happening here? As an animal of flight a horse will normally run away from pressure but you can teach him that instead of thinking 'away' from people, he thinks 'towards' people at the moment you are putting him under pressure. We are teaching the horse to replace his Emergency Plan A – 'run away' – with Plan B – 'stand still and look'.

Step 4:
Let the horse move around in a circle again and use pressure to get him to turn his quarters out.

When this happens, make yourself smaller and move backwards and slap your thigh twice. The horse should walk towards you.

Step 5:
Stand in front of the horse and take up a slight pressure on the lead rope. As soon as the horse moves in your direction stop the pressure. If the horse moves away move his hips over again and use step 4 to ask him to come to you.

Step 6:
Standing relaxed.
Once you have successfully completed the exercises and got your horse to stand, position yourself next to his shoulder and, using step

When the horse reaches you give him a rest and let him relax.

4

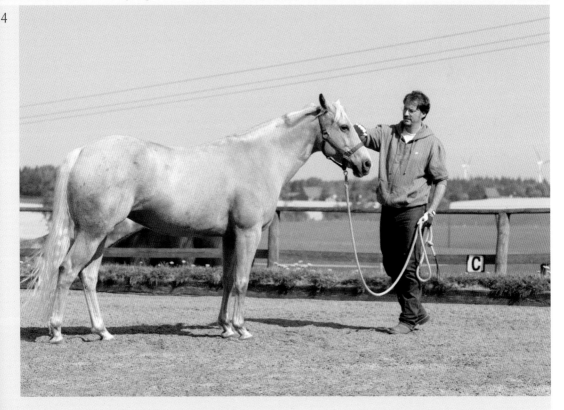

Step 6: Use the exercise you have already learned to ask the horse to lower his head.

Allow the horse to stand like this for as long as possible.

3 from exercise HE3, ask him to lower his head. Whenever the horse tries to lift his head, ask him to lower it again. You are trying to get the horse to stand with his head lowered. In this way he has to accept that he can't just look around at everything. At the same time he will relax if he keeps his head held low. This acceptance of his field of vision being restricted will also help you when you start working on establishing a contact.

CE2:
Is anyone there?

Tap the horse's cheekbone and take up a gentle contact with the lead rope. If the horse blinks or shuts his eyes this is a normal reaction.

What should it look like? You should be standing next to your horse. If he looks anywhere else, all you need to do is to lift you hand and wave it. Your horse should turn his head towards you.

Stand next to your horse and wave your hand slightly, on a level with his head. I guarantee that your horse will either not react or will turn his head away from you. Now tap him gently just under his cheekbone with one finger and at the same time take up the rope slightly. The horse will try to raise his head, turn it to the side or other similar evasions. This is quite normal for an animal of flight trying to get away from what is irritating or scaring him. Persist, though, until the horse turns his head towards you (it will happen eventually). At this moment stop and stroke the horse over and around his eye. If you always work in this order a wave of your hand should suffice to get the horse to turn his head and wish to push his head into your hand. I always compare this exercise to when someone taps you on your shoulder from behind – your concentration moves to that spot and you turn around.

What has happened here? Through the exercise we have increased the stimulus – first

As soon as the horse turns to look at you, you must immediately stop tapping and release the contact on the rope. Stroke your horse across his forehead.

waving, then tapping. As already mentioned, every horse will react to strong stimuli by taking evasive action. He is 'thinking' away from people. With this exercise, however, he learns to concentrate on his handler instead, and despite feeling under more pressure turns towards rather than away from her. By using the learning behaviour of our horses (operant conditioning) we can teach a horse to show behaviour that is exactly the opposite of what an animal of flight would normally do.

The stimulus doesn't cause the horse to run away, but rather to approach. The effect of this little exercise is enormous. As well as improving the horse's ability to concentrate, another pleasant side effect is that the horse is easier to tack up and is more ready to have his head touched. Leading should also get better, because the horse will be 'thinking' towards your hand and is more likely to follow it with his head.

HANDY HINT

During calmness training we put a horse in a situation from which he wants to run away but he learns instead to focus on his handler. It is not a question of whether he wants to take off, but when. If you are unsure of what you are doing and not practised in the use of your emergency exercise (Plan B), and you take the pressure away, your horse will take evasive action and will soon learn to take off. You don't have to worry about lunge lines, whips or other things that may slow down your reactions. Using pressure you are able to control much of your horse's behaviour, but always be prepared. Practise this 'look at me and stand still' exercise a great deal.

CE3:
Stimulus at halt

Horses should let themselves be touched all over their body – lack of this acceptance reflects how much of the flight animal still remains. If there are places on his body that he hasn't 'given' you yet, problems will always arise because his trust hasn't been well enough established. Furthermore, it is important for your vet to able to touch your horse everywhere.

Step1:
Begin by stroking your horse all over, starting from his back.

At first use a whip so that you can stand at a safe distance. If your horse tries to get away from you at any point note this and start to work around the surrounding area. Use a tactic of advance and retreat, to get closer to the particular point before the horse can react. If despite this he moves, stay where you were until he stands still again and then stop (remember the way a horse learns). If the horse moves away too fast then stop him using your emergency exercise and start over again.

Step 2:
Stand next to your saddled horse and slap your hand on your thigh. Your horse should stand still, neither turning away nor walking off. If he shows either of these responses try to maintain your position next to the horse by moving with him. If this isn't possible, turn the horse round and after he comes to a halt put your hand on his wither – this helps you to keep to your own position – and go back to where you were and start again. (You can see that the approach is always the same.)

When you can do this, you can start to jump up and down on the spot. Tap the saddle

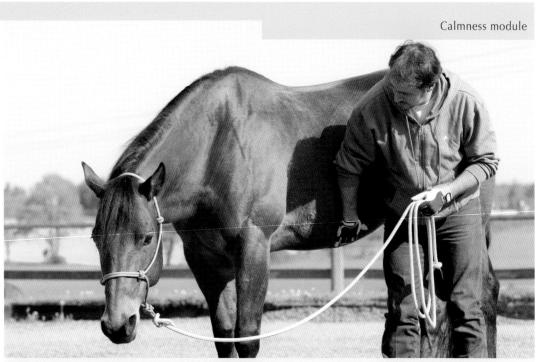

When running your hands over your horse, it helps if he has dropped his head before you start.
It is then easier for you to tell if he doesn't like something because he will lift his head.

The horse has to learn to accept not only your hand.
You should also be able to touch a horse anywhere with a variety of objects or aids.

CE4: Having enough reach is important if you want to work with a moving horse. Never tie anything to the horse or the saddle to get him used to it. There are other ways.

and lift one of your legs as if you were going to get on. Gradually increase the amount of pressure and be sensible but not over-cautious.

CE4:
Stimulus when moving

While many horses will let themselves be touched all over when stationary, they act very differently once they are moving. However, in these circumstances especially we need to be sure that a horse will accept something touching him. You certainly wouldn't want to be taken by surprise if, when hacking out, a branch got stuck in your horse's tail and banged up against his hocks. The surprise may be bigger than you think if he takes off with you. To practise this

I would recommend using a collapsible fishing rod about 5 metres in length (the type that you can take apart or fold down) bought from a fishing supplies shop. Remove the first and last sections of the rod. When you work your horse on a small circle you can touch him on the neck, back and hindlegs with the rod.

The approach should always be the same: if the horse gets faster, use the process of moving his hips to slow him down and bring him back to a halt. If he doesn't change his pace then take the rod away again. It is also useful to let the rod bob up and down on his back a bit as this will start to simulate the movement of a rider on his back. You should work your way over his back, croup and hindlegs using this method.

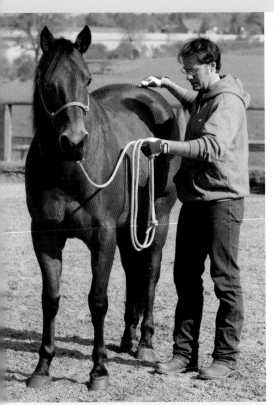

CE5: This exercise shows the importance of timing. Here too the horse needs to be focused on you and must not run away.

CE5:
Backing up

Stand next to your horse, lift your hand as if to wave and begin to pat him on his croup.

Continue to pat with more force until he begins to move. A light pull on the rope helps to give the horse direction. Provided that he goes forwards or steps over with the inside hind, increase the degree of turn through the rope. At some stage the inside hind will not move forwards, but backwards. At this moment stop straight away. Your horse is starting to focus on you and doesn't want to run away. When your horse is standing still again, scratch him at the base of his tail. In this exercise your attention is on his inside hindleg. When you pat him he should move it back.

CE6:
Rope exercise at halt and when moving

Stand level with the horse's shoulder and swing your rope repeatedly over his back, croup and

CE6: Swing the rope over his back. It doesn't matter if it hits his belly on the other side. After all, your horse shouldn't run away if the stirrup hits him on his side.

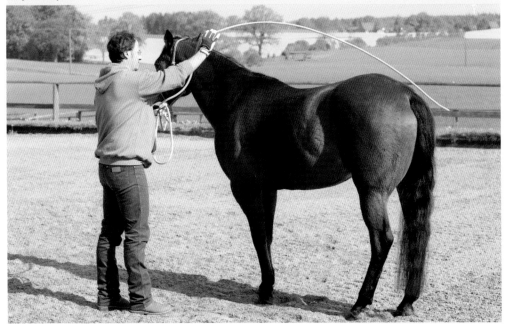

A horse's response is greater when he is moving. Be prepared to slow the horse down by moving his quarters.

hindlegs. He should remain standing still. You can try this exercise as well while the horse is being led on a small circle. By using your ability to control his hips you should be able to control the situation at any time and slow his movement down if necessary. Apart from this use the same approach and Plan B. At this stage a new element comes into play – the rope enters the horse's blind spot and once over his back appears in the field of vision of his other eye. (Refer to the section on dealing with stimuli, page 30)

HANDY HINT

Approach to take: In all exercises when standing still, the horse should stand in one place. If the exercise is carried out when the horse is moving, the horse should be aware of the stimulus but continue as normal. Nearly all horses, though, consider running away. For this reason I always try, at the start, to use this movement to get the horse to stand and listen to me (refer to Plan B, page 85). Only when I can see that the horse is prepared to stand still do I ask him to move off again. Only then can I be sure that the horse is moving on without those thoughts of flight. Besides, it is always sensible to have a

plan ready in case of emergency, before he decides to take off. There will always be times, however, when this doesn't work, especially if there are other sources of stimulation (for example horses galloping about in the field next to you). In situations such as this I go back to my basic exercise (leading on a circle), asking him to move his quarters over to keep him soft, preventing him from trying to take off and getting his rear end out of my own danger zone. Once I have got him back under control I will stop him, give him a short rest and then start the exercise over again.

Don't hide the flag with your body. If the horse doesn't register it with either his ear or eye, an even stronger reaction may yet come. Many horses take some time to notice this one.

Visual stimuli: switching from one eye to the other

As already mentioned on page 31, this ability to 'switch' eyes is one of the most important things that a horse needs to learn. Many a rider, when trying to get on her horse, has fallen off when her leg has suddenly appeared on the horse's off side out of nowhere. Another example of this is the sleeve of a jacket appearing when you are trying to put on a coat when in the saddle.

CE7: Flag work

A flag (or plastic bag, preferably white, blue or yellow, tied to a whip) is useful for getting a horse used to things like this.

Step 1:
Walk on a small circle and simply carry the flag with you. Observe your horse to see whether he reacts differently with either eye and whether he shows any signs of taking avoidance measures. Use a distance that you know your horse will accept. Use the flag to ask the horse to move his hips, so that he comes to a halt. At the moment he stops, hide the flag behind your back. (Plan B says to him: 'If you are worried about something, look at it and stop and then it will disappear.')

Use the flag to ask the horse to yield his quarters as in the basic exercises. Doing this should get a controlled reaction from your horse.

Dusty clearly becomes tense when the bag is behind or above him. He can be stopped easily, though.

After practising only a few times the horse starts to get more relaxed (compare the horse's topline in both photos).

Step 2:

Repeat the exercise but hold the flag noticeably higher and angled over the horse. Use a turn to ask him to halt. Only when the horse is about to stop of his own volition, ask him to continue to walk on until he takes several relaxed steps with the flag in the same place over him.

Using the fishing rod we can put a slightly greater and safer distance between us and the horse when practising teaching the horse to switch eyes with objects moving over his back. This area is particularly important for riders.

Step 3:

Stand in line with the saddle area and with a greater distance between you and your horse take the rod with the bag attached and move it over his back into his field of vision on the other side. This distance is necessary in case the horse decides to take off. If this happens leave the rod on the horse's back and turn him into a halt. Only then take the rod away.

Step 4:

Train this on a circle with the horse in walk and then in trot.

This is how the end result should look: Dusty continues to walk and is aware of the flag but without getting tense.

Step 4: Dusty reacts in an exemplary manner: he keeps his eye on the bag but continues to walk calmly forwards.

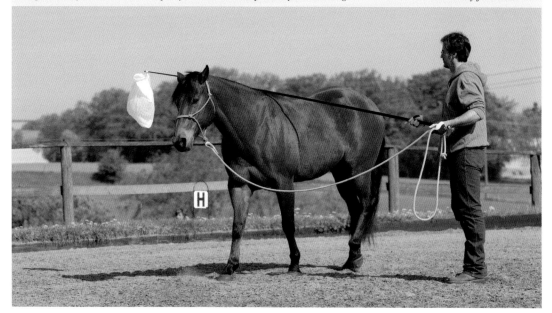

Step 5: In this exercise Dusty is running away from the stimulus that is following him.

By asking him to yield through his hip I can control the situation and bring him to a halt.

After he has stood and looked at it I take the bag away and step back in order to take the pressure off Dusty. This is another example of advance and retreat.

Step 5:

Chasing. Let the rod slide down behind the horse on to the ground so that the plastic bag is now 'chasing' the horse. If your horse gets faster turn him round again. The goal is for your horse to continue without changing pace in a relaxed manner even if the rod touches his back legs.

Step 6:

Hold the rod in front of the horse and let the horse follow the rod. This is good practice to counter shying.

Dusty looks rather unhappy but accepts the presence of the bag bravely.

In the saddle

Most problems occur in the saddle because the rider becomes a source of stimulus; furthermore, there are other external factors that appear as additional stimuli. In the training exercises described so far the horse has learnt to cope better with both. As my main exercise in the saddle I use the all-purpose exercise shown on page 107, where for once I use my legs much more strongly than necessary but expect the horse to stay soft. Likewise, I use this exercise to work on concentration – whenever the horse is distracted I begin to flap my legs gently against him until his attention is directed back to me.

In the case of other stimuli that are to one side or the other (for example a jacket hung over the fence) I use the following approach. I flex the horse as a matter of principle in the opposite direction to the danger because it makes it harder for him to run out through his shoulder to get away from it. The usual reaction is to look at the danger and then get away through the other shoulder. I put the horse at a distance that he will accept (grey zone) and at which I

If a horse has already learnt to stop as soon as you hold a whip in front of him then this can lead to misunderstandings. With a little practice and patience though, the horse should be able to learn the difference.

can get him to go past the apparently dangerous object safely. As he walks past it I ask him to approach the source of danger by leg yielding. If you have a helper on the ground she can create visual or audible stimuli. Meanwhile I make certain that my horse continues to walk forwards. If he gets upset or excited I turn the horse to face the danger and ask him to stand, at which point my helper must stop or hide the source of danger – the principle should always be the same.

Collection and
shoulder module

The shoulders are one of the most important parts of the horse that you should be able to influence when riding, a fact that is given far too little significance. By nature horses will put more weight on their forehand than their hindquarters, which is viewed as their engine and source of energy. When being ridden, horses try to maintain this weight distribution, which makes it difficult for us to get the shoulders into the position that we strive to achieve. What is the significance of this?

In every exercise the hips and shoulders are related to each other in a specific way (shoulder in, travers, circles, etc.). At the same time it is clearly easier for the horse to move his hips, so he tends to align his hips with his shoulders. Instead of shoulder in, the horse tends to work 'hips out'.

If you try to ride travers, it is often the case that the shoulder will move off the outside track. With nearly every horse, when working on a 10-metre circle you can see how, although you can flex him slightly to the inside, instead of being ridden into the outside rein the hindquarters will fall slightly to the outside and the horse will swing out through his shoulder. The list of cases such as this is never ending.

In my opinion, the main problem when riding lies in the fact that we are not able to exert enough control over the horse's shoulders. While we can, to an extent, overlook the problem of the shoulders being slightly out of alignment in relation to the hips, in collection it becomes more of an issue. For collection the horse needs be prepared to be loose in his shoulder. This set of training exercises is designed to give you more control over the shoulders so as to be able to position them more accurately.

RW6:
Lateral exercises

Step 1:
This exercise is a direct follow-on from RW2. Ride a small circle, put your inside leg slightly back and ask the horse to move his hips slightly to the side. The neck should be flexed slightly to the inside and the horse should be soft through his poll. As soon as the quarters can swing around with ease, rest the inside rein with greater pressure on the wither (but don't pull back) and allow the horse to move his shoulder a step to the outside. Your leg controls his hips; the reins control the horse's shoulder.

Step 2:
In step 1 you have created a lot of impulsion by moving the quarters. Now you need to reduce this step by step and allow the quarters to move

INFO

For your own sake it is important to be able to develop a feeling of whether an exercise is being done correctly. Whether a horse is on a good contact or is leaning on your hand can be noticed quickly, but how do you know whether the horse is walking properly and is stopping as he should? How does it feel if a horse falls on to his forehand?

A comparison with driving a car might help us. You have all probably felt how a car reacts when you brake: the front lowers and you are tipped slightly forwards. When braking at high speed this is much more noticeable but think about what it is like if the car is only just moving and you brake lightly. This is exactly what it feels like when a horse falls on to his forehand (shoulders) when you ask him to walk or

halt. When you drive off, however, the front of a car lifts up slightly. This is exactly what a good upward transition should feel like. If you think about this transference of weight when driving, you will quickly recognise it when on your horse. For me, a good contact feels like good power steering. I can feel the tyres on the road through the corners. As soon as I have to really hold on to the steering wheel firmly, the feeling of the power steering disappears. A good contact is exactly the same. If, on the other hand, the horse falls behind the contact it feels the same as when I am driving round a bend and I lose the feeling of having a contact with the road. The steering suddenly gets very light and I don't have my car fully under control.

Step 1: My leg keeps the horse's hindleg active and the rein shows the shoulder the way. As long as the outside rein stays loose, I get a four-beat movement. This is acceptable for now.

just one stride over, before asking the shoulder to do the same.

RW7:
Work on a circle

Step 1:
Ride the horse on a contact on a volte with him flexed correctly to the inside. Now straighten up your horse by giving the inside rein slightly and taking the outside rein up a bit more – both reins should be held close to the withers, so that they lie on the shoulder. If your horse tries to fall to the outside, then use your outside leg to contain the movement. Go back and forth between inside flexion and straightness. You can make it easier for you and your horse by setting out cones to mark the inner and outer circles to show the horse the way.

Step 2: By taking more of a contact in the outside rein I get movement on two tracks. Only take a stronger contact if the horse stays soft in his mouth.

Step 3: When turning with outside flexion, horses have to learn that they must allow themselves to be led through their shoulders and on a contact with the rein.

Step 2:

Flex your horse to the outside so that you can see his outside eye. The horse should stay on the circle. If keeping the rein against his shoulder is not enough to keep him on the circle, you can also allow your outside leg to move back on to the girth and support it. If this doesn't work, put more weight down through your inside stirrup. It is important to remember the order in which you give the aids. The horse should accept the rein.

Step 3:

As soon as you can keep your horse on the volte with outside flexion, use the outside rein to put more pressure on the shoulder and ask the horse to turn to the inside. Your outside leg should be placed loosely on the girth. End this exercise by changing the rein but using the correct bend

and you should automatically have good inside flexion with a free inside shoulder. You are thus riding a figure of eight.

You could also try riding this exercise: right rein with inside flexion – change the flexion – turn with left flexion – move on to the left rein (you already have left flexion).

Steps 4 and 5:

Instead of outside flexion, in step 4 ride the horse straight – i.e. with no flexion to either side. In step 5 maintain the inside flexion. From now on your inside leg (or the inside rein) is responsible for the inside flexion and the outside rein is what asks the horse to turn. You are now working using the correct method. At this stage an important development takes place: the horse starts to work between the reins, rather than, as up until now, working the shoulder off

Steps 4 and 5: A correct turn with inside flexion is very difficult. The horse must soften to the outside rein, but also accept the inside rein as restricting any tipping to the inside. Only now is he really working 'between the reins'.

one rein or the other. This means that the inside rein stops the horse from falling to the inside while the outside rein controls the bend. This only can only work when he carries more weight through his quarters.

Why did we use outside flexion?

As already described, horses by nature tend to put more weight on to their shoulders than through their quarters. It is not really possible to ask the shoulder for inside flexion if the horse is putting all his weight down through his shoulder. Using outside flexion makes it easier to influence the shoulder. Furthermore, outside flexion can be used as a means of correction; if the horse doesn't turn correctly when flexed to the inside, you can use outside flexion in order to have more control over the shoulder.

HANDY HINT

There are always horses that find this exercise difficult. In these cases use your surroundings to help you. Cut the corners of your arena off with a rope (at 45 degrees) and ride your horse through the corners with outside flexion. Also try leg yielding down the outside track. Often the problem lies with the shoulder being kept too tight due to the horse's back being too tense. This is why it is important that the exercises for the shoulders are only tried after completing the foundation module so that the horse is already warmed up and relaxed. Trouble with balance can also be the cause of problems, especially when the exercises don't work in trot.

Introduce the rein back by asking the horse to move his quarters over.

When the inside foreleg is stationary but the horse continues to move his quarters round you will notice that the inside shoulder has lightened.

RW8:
Rein back

The exercises up until now have concentrated on asking the shoulders to move to the side. Use of the reins on one side asks the relevant shoulder to soften and ensures that the horse doesn't lean on that shoulder. Now, however, the horse has to transfer his weight back from the shoulder to the hindquarters.

Step 1:

In exercise RW2 we used a turn on the forehand to make the inside foreleg the pivot for the turn, and as a result the horse has kept this leg in the same place and we have thus stopped forward movement. If you continued to move the quarters round you would see that the inside shoulder lightened and the horse would tend to want to move the inside fore back a step. At this moment you need to sit deeper in the saddle and take up a contact through both reins until the horse goes back a step. This is the first step towards a rein back with a light shoulder. The horse already knows this as an in-hand exercise (HE2). When starting this exercise it is a good idea to be aware that most horses try not to move the inside fore so that they can lean on it – it's a bit like trying to take away someone's walking stick. Correct a horse that stands still by asking him to move his quarters again and never by pulling back more on the reins. A helper on the ground can also support you in this exercise.

This is the moment to ask for the rein back. Here you can clearly see how Sciona tries to keep her weight on the inside foreleg.

As soon as the inside fore is in the air loosen your contact. The horse then learns to soften to the pressure by lifting the appropriate leg.

HANDY HINT

Have you followed the basic principles?

Given that this book is all about teaching the horse specific sequences of movements, and you have to pay attention to lots of different things at the same time, it is very easy to get totally confused, especially when starting out. For this reason it is probably helpful between training sessions to re-read the sections covering the theory of what we are trying to do and go back over your 'checklist' in your mind. Have you got your memory card in your head? Do you know when to end a particular lesson so that the horse gets the right idea? Is your timing spot on?

Step 2:
As soon as your horse can take several steps starting from both reins without showing resistance, reduce the amount of turn used. Ride a volte and sit deep in the saddle, letting the quarters move over only one step. The inside rein should cause the inside shoulder to lift. This is one of the most important aims of this module – to teach the horse that after the turn on the forehand there is a moment of collection, with the horse lightening in front to carry out the rein back and transferring his weight back on to his quarters. The outside rein simply has to maintain a soft contact. If the horse moves on to the outside shoulder instead of coming to a halt, then you should take up more contact on the outside rein. If this isn't enough,

ask the quarters to step over by using your inside leg until the horse lightens and moves back. Don't be surprised if at the start this exercise looks totally different – the horse will understand the sequence of movements being asked for relatively quickly.

Step 3:

Once the horse is responding to both reins when they are taken up separately, without having to turn him, it is time to take up both reins simultaneously. Ride forwards on a light contact and sit deep in the saddle. Take both reins up slightly strongly and ask for several steps of rein back.

RW9
The clock exercise

The following exercise is one of my favourites for the shoulders. Using this can really help to lighten the horse to the aids. There is only one problem – you have to make sure that the use of your reins is synchronised with the movement of your horse's front legs. It can take some time until you can ride this exercise with ease but it is worth the effort. The basic idea is that you have to imagine the face of a clock. Your horse is moving towards 12 o'clock. Take both reins up as the left foreleg steps forwards so that you have a contact when the right foreleg is about to leave the ground. At this moment move both reins slightly to the right and place the right fore on 1 o'clock. As soon as the right fore touches the ground give with both reins so that you don't restrict the left leg in stepping forwards. Ideally you should repeat this sequence twice in a row. When the horse steps on to 1 o'clock (or 11 o'clock for the left fore) move on to 2 or 10 o'clock. You can thus work back to 6 o'clock. Here you can achieve a rein back in which the legs are well placed.

From 3 (and 9) o'clock the horse will stop moving forwards, and 4 or 8 o'clock is the place to begin a spin in Western riding. As well as control over the shoulder, this exercise requires a high degree of coordination on the part of the horse, and his balance will show a lasting improvement (refer also to the module on balance and coordination).

Just before the inside foreleg leaves the ground the contact should be established.

CAUTION

The 'reward trap'

It is always the little things that catch us out. This might be the 'reward trap', as one of my pupils found out. We were teaching her horse the spin (a fast turn on the quarters as ridden in Western riding) and the horse was making good progress. After a week, however, the horse got slower rather than faster. The rider always took off the pressure at the right time: in other words, as the horse was going faster. After stopping, however, she would scratch his wither as praise for good work. At this moment she was rewarding her horse for stopping (which was the last action before the praise), and this behaviour was becoming established. This is just one of the small traps in training.

Ask the leg to move to the side with the rein and then let the contact go as the leg is put down. You can see from this photo how difficult Dusty finds it to lift this leg up – one reason why he is also hard to collect.

RW10:
The all-purpose exercise

This exercise can be integrated into all of the modules because it serves to improve collection and softness as well as a horse's calm way of working. I begin doing this quite early on in a horse's education (at least from RW4) and give myself plenty of time.

Step 1:
Take up a light contact on the reins and begin to tap both legs gently against the horse, on the girth. Your horse should be stationary. Wait until he drops his head slightly and at this moment give with both reins.

What do I do if …
… the horse moves forwards: Take up more contact on the reins and prevent the forward movement.
… the horse moves back: Release the reins briefly, drive him forwards and catch this forward movement through the reins. Some horses get very upset and the backward movement will get worse. In this situation I move straight on to step 3.
… the horse doesn't react at all: Lift one hand while you are flapping your legs (RW3) and

The sequence of steps for the walk. When moving into walk many horses move their centre of gravity forwards...

... and fall on to the forehand, as is easily seen in this photo.

allow the horse to take the rein down. Repeat the exercise until this correction isn't needed anymore.

Step 2:
Ride three steps forward, halt and let the horse drop his head, at the same time gently tapping with both legs on the girth. Ride forward again, halt and repeat the sequence.

Step 3:
Now ride on a small circle and repeat the exercise until the horse softens easily. Any correction can be done using RW3 or by asking for the quarters to move over (RW2). The horse should stay in walk. Watch out that your horse doesn't go either faster or slower, otherwise he will learn to associate your leg with a change of speed.

Step 4:
Vary the contact. Until now you have always given the rein forward clearly so that the horse was encouraged to stretch forwards and down. We have ensured that the horse stretches, but have not yet achieved true direct (or longitudinal) flexion, in other words the horse stretching along the length of his back, straight but on a contact. Now try giving the rein only about 10 centimetres. The horse should stretch down into the bridle, meet the bit and accept the contact. When this is working well, limit the amount that you give to only

With the left rein (in this case) you have to hold the shoulder, or even possibly flex the horse slightly to the left.

After this correction the horse is clearly straighter. You can, however, see from the tilting of his head that he is still tense.

a few centimetres and hold the contact for a few seconds, then give him more rein and allow the horse to stretch down into the bridle. Above all it is important that you create a desire to stretch down before you work on the contact. Only then will you achieve direct flexion with the horse working through his back in a correct outline. A forced outline is easily recognised: if the horse's head lifts after giving with the rein the horse was tense through his back and he was forced into the outline by the rider's hand.

Step 5:

This step requires a degree of routine and a sensitive touch, because we now want to work on the shoulder. The further you progress in this module, the better the results will be. In walk, ask the horse to stretch down into a firm contact and ask through your seat for the halt while continuing to ask with your legs. If the desired response hasn't already happened here at the latest, your horse may show signs of resistance because he will try to do something quite different to get away from doing what you are asking him to do.

If he doesn't want to slow down, just persist and wait. After about 10 seconds, halt him by asking him to move his quarters and ask him for a rein back (RW8). This serves to get the horse to soften and lift his shoulder and doesn't represent a punishment.

Many horses will also start to fall out through one shoulder. Ask the horse for counter-bend and continue to tap with your legs.

Other horses will begin to swing their hindquarters because their front end is contained but they can't or won't yet be able to carry more weight through their quarters. Place your leg on the appropriate side slightly further back (continuing to tap) and correct the swinging out. If the horse won't accept your leg then you may need to go back to exercise RW2.

Some horses will begin to get 'sticky' and in this case put your legs slightly further back and push them forwards again.

Step 6:

Do this in trot as well as on straight lines. If it doesn't work when riding straight, go back on to a circle that you make smaller and smaller, until you can do it.

The last step can be made easier by forming a pathway using cones that offers the horse support to either side (refer to the balance module on page 119).

The general rule is always to stop tapping with your legs and give with the rein as soon as the horse shows the desired response. RW3 will always help to get the horse to give to you. If you have tightened up yourself and stalemate has developed with your horse, go back to RW8. Later this leg tapping (which will eventually reduce to vibrating or rubbing) will cause the horse to stretch down into a contact, when working laterally or even when reining back.

From this point on you should notice that every exercise will start to improve. Halting especially (RW8) will become more energetic – the horse is in direct flexion, you sit into the saddle and put your legs on. The horse should lift his forehand, sit slightly on his quarters and maintain the contact. You should now be able to use half-halts more effectively. These should be given as the leg is about to land on the ground, not when it is in the air!

The same applies to the use of your legs. Because we always take up the reins first, we are training this as the first signal to listen to. Using your legs actively against your horse's sides, as you have been doing, should become unnecessary because he should go into an outline when you take up the reins. If you want to establish this leg tapping as a signal (for example in Western tests where a long rein is used throughout) you will need to reverse the timing of the signals as soon as the horse responds well to your hands. First put the leg on, then the rein. In addition, I use this tapping to get the horse's attention. I observe his ears – when he has them pricked forwards and is concentrating on something or someone else I tap my legs on him until he turns an ear back to me to show that he is listening to me.

Applying the exercises

A7:
Figure of eight with change of flexion

Ride a volte on the left rein with flexion to the inside. Change the rein without a change of flexion (circle to the right with left flexion). Now flex the horse to the inside. Again change the rein without changing the flexion (circle to the left with right flexion). Flex to the inside and start again.

A8:
Figure of eight without change of flexion

Ride a figure of eight but when you change reins do not change the flexion.

A9:
Travers

Travers can also be worked on using outside flexion. Ride down the long side of your arena about 2 metres in from the track (for example on the left rein). Flex your horse to the left and ask him back to the track through the shoulder. The shoulder should get back to the track before the quarters. Keeping the shoulders on the track, continue to use your inside leg (left) and let your right leg be passive to support the movement. Your horse is likely to try to move his quarters over to the track automatically. You should, however, concentrate on having his shoulders reach the track first. By doing this exercise, travers will start to develop by itself.

A10:
Stop sign

Ride on a straight line with the horse straight. Turn the horse one step to the side and ask him to go straight again. We are not looking for bend or flexion. If he won't go straight and wants to bend you have to 'counter steer'. You are therefore making a stop sign out of a circle. When riding this, always pick a point to ride to so that you can immediately see if you are deviating from the chosen path and can correct it.

Balance and coordination module

Note from the translator: In German the author uses two words – Balance and Gleichgewicht – to differentiate between two concepts that the author wishes to highlight dealing with balance. In English the translation of both words is usually balance but to differentiate here we will use 'external balance' and 'internal balance', and the difference will become clear in the definitions.

When standing still, a horse is balanced when his centre of gravity lies within his weight-bearing area. At halt this area is marked out by his four feet. When he is moving, the horse's centre of gravity shifts as a result of external forces (for example the centrifugal force on a circle). The smaller the weight-bearing area becomes, the more accurately the centre of gravity has to be positioned within it, so that the horse doesn't lose this equilibrium and fall or stumble. As long as a horse can move his

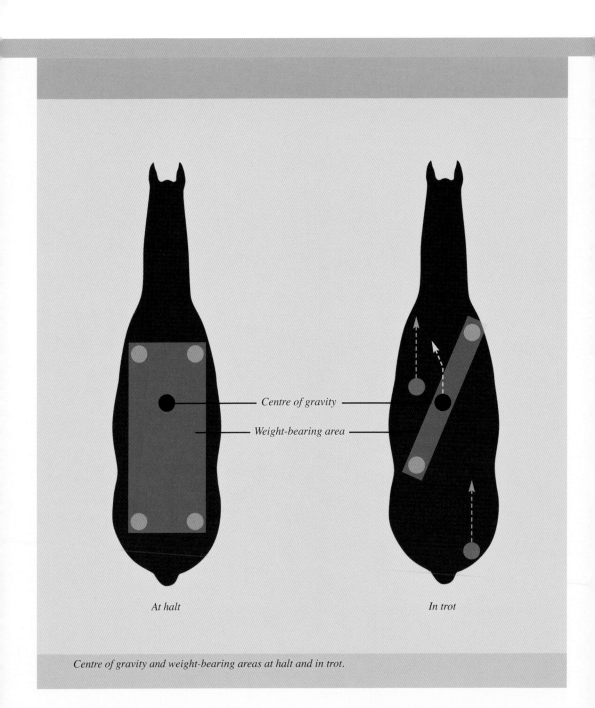

Centre of gravity

Weight-bearing area

At halt

In trot

Centre of gravity and weight-bearing areas at halt and in trot.

centre of gravity within his weight-bearing area he has found his balance. If the centre of gravity falls outside this area, the horse is imbalanced. To counter this he will quickly move a leg in such a way as to create a new weight-bearing area under the centre of gravity, or position another part of his body (usually the head or neck) so that the centre of gravity is moved back into the weight-bearing area. In other words a correction is made externally (i.e. physically). For movement itself, the centre of gravity has to be moved away from the weight-bearing area, albeit minimally and in a controlled fashion. This movement can be slowed down or stopped at any time. External measures used to correct balance may not be visible (for example when we use our hands in the pockets of our jacket to help us balance). With horses who don't have a good sense of balance, their centre of gravity moves over the weight-bearing area in a more extreme fashion, so they have to take more extreme corrective measures to avoid falling over. Until this point, external and internal balance are the same.

With internal balance, however, the weight-bearing area becomes noticeably smaller and the horse's external balance becomes more precarious. What sounds at first like something that has negative connotations is necessary for good riding, however, because it makes a horse more mobile and agile and better able to work off the aids. In addition, the reduced area used to carry weight enables the horse to move his back in such a way that he is better able to carry a rider.

The solution: Three main components are responsible for external and internal balance. The centre of balance works in combination with the vestibular organ in the ears, the eyes, and receptors in the muscles that tell the horse where his body is and how he is moving it (these so-called proprioceptors ensure that we can place our finger on our nose with our eyes shut). External balance starts from these receptors and a perception of one's own body. A foal starts to develop this awareness instinctively by playing in the field, and these first few months are enormously important for the development of a good sense of balance as the horse grows up.

Our training therefore takes place in three stages:

• Teaching a better perception of the body
• Establishing external balance
• Developing an internal sense of balance.

Teaching a horse perception of its own body

Taking advantage of different surfaces is the easiest and most effective method to train this awareness of the body. When riding out you should try to ride through mud and puddles and on many different materials, as well as using slopes or narrow paths that make a horse use his body. Hacking out is not just a good way of relaxing the horse and rider but is also an important part of the training process, especially when you can go 'off road'. Even a simple jumping pole can be used to improve proprioception.

If you look carefully enough you will find lots of small challenges hidden around for horse and rider. Why not ask your horse to rein back up or down a hill or slope? Why not lead a horse across a trailer ramp or ask him to go backwards into a trailer, or through a door? Any work done with the horse going backwards, or any variation from the surfaces he is used to, is a good exercise. It is, however, important that you take things slowly and consider whether the obstacle you are about to attempt is safe for both horse and handler.

Pole work

The aim here is to lead a horse step by step over a single pole. He should put only one foot at a time over the pole and then after a brief pause move it back. Provided that the horse isn't holding his head extremely low, he can't see the pole. The slow 'placing' of each individual leg is not what he is used to doing, and so this movement has to be undertaken consciously. It gets particularly difficult when the horse is asked to move his hindlegs backwards over a pole.

A horse usually has less awareness of his quarters than is needed to step over a pole that

The hindleg lifted high is a clear sign that Lilly can't yet read the situation. She is still lacking a clear awareness of her body. Horses like this often also try to push their handler out of the way to get out of the situation.

can't be seen. Horses with poor body awareness often get very upset and may try to take evasive action. It is important to work through this initial work thoroughly because this foundation will be put to the test with harder challenges as the work develops. Every time the horse's leg hits one of the poles it is informing his body about the position of that leg, which in turn activates the body's receptors. This exercise also teaches the horse to move his legs without shifting his centre of gravity too much. For this reason it is a very good way of schooling the horse's external balance.

Establishing external balance

With horses that have a problem with their sense of balance, it is possible to see from the way they walk that their centre of gravity is clearly outside their weight-bearing area. First the body rocks forward, and only after this is the leg moved forwards. In particular, large horses with lots of impulsion tend to have difficulties with their balance. Even at a walk they will be running to catch up with their centre of gravity, and in trot they will be clearly seen to be moving too fast. They will also often become overbent.

Horses such as these have to learn to move their legs faster so that they are better able to find their weight-bearing area (refer to pole work on page 116). While the legs need to move faster, however, it is better for his balance if the horse slows himself down, especially in trot. These horses don't necessarily engage more through their quarters or track up more, rather they just tip forwards and get faster and faster as they try to catch up with their centre of gravity. The following exercises are intended to teach

the horse to learn to balance himself. We have already talked about many of the related riding methods that can be used when problems with balance are being experienced. They are well suited for horses with real balance problems, as well as for youngsters. Such horses may not yet accept the aids and there is a risk that the horse will start to become tense and block the aids. For this reason the visual aids used are very important to assist the horse in learning, without him becoming reliant on them.

Cone forest

Scatter cones around the arena in no particular pattern. Lunge your horse through this 'forest', changing your own position constantly so that the horse has to try continuously to find a new route. The cones should be far enough apart that the horse can't just avoid them as a group and won't try to jump over them, but must be close enough to force the horse to try and go through them and to cause a change of direction. This simple exercise schools the horse's attention and his eye-leg coordination, as well as his balance. You can of course ride this exercise as well, but on a loose rein so you don't interfere with the horse. For the rider this is a good exercise too, because she has to follow the unpredictable movement of her horse. Before you try it though, make sure that you are secure in your seat. Most horses will adapt their speed and often slow down. If you have problems controlling speed when lungeing, position groups of cones around the circle to help to slow down a rushing horse. In addition the movement the horse makes in getting around and through the cones will help to loosen muscles, and this exercise can be particularly effective when used with gaited horses (such as Icelandic ponies) that are having problems with pacing.

Here too you can see that the horse is lacking awareness of her body. The tension that results can be clearly seen in the hindleg, the tension through the neck and the entire top line.

The result after a few minutes. The mare is clearly more relaxed and is walking with a much more natural outline through the cone forest.

The cones laid to the inside and outside offer Lilly a visual 'crutch'.
This helps her to learn to balance on a circle.

Cone circle

It is also easy to create a circle using the cones. The aim is that your horse learns to balance when on a circle. The cones act as a visual boundary without having a direct 'mechanical' effect on the horse (when compared with side reins). At the start the horse will be unsteady and may waver, will lose his outline and is likely to vary the speed. Allow the horse time to sort himself out. With time he will get slower and the head will drop. At this stage it is natural for the horse to have an outside bend through his neck. Only step in if the horse falls to the inside or outside through the cones: as long as the horse stays between the cones don't interfere, with one exception: if your horse goes faster and faster and tries to canter, you must bring him back to halt. Following this, ask him

to trot a couple of circles then bring him back to walk. Play about with the size of the circle and the width of the gap between the two sets of cones.

If you try riding this exercise it is important not to apply the aids constantly because the horse has to learn to find his own balance and not rely on your aids to achieve this exercise.

Working on an oval

If when on a circle your horse tends to bend to the outside and puts more weight down through his inside shoulder, and you let him work like this for any length of time, this will become established and it will make future work more difficult. If this is the case then divide your circle into two half circles and 'pull' them a few metres apart. You have now formed an oval

In the 6-metre long straight section of the oval, the horse should be straight and stretch forwards and down.

instead to flex his head to the outside, put his weight on to his shoulder and use his long back muscles to carry the rider. The exercises detailed above form a transition. The development of this internal sense of balance must be influenced by the rider. For this reason we need to combine the patterns used above with the following ridden exercises.

Cone circle

Step 1:
Ride on a circle and begin to ask the horse to stretch down into a contact using RW3 and RW4. Ask for inside flexion again and again until the horse will stay on the circle on a long rein on a light contact. Once in the right outline you can let him continue on for some time because it is good to reinforce this sequence.

Step 2:
Now start to alternate between inside and outside flexion (RW7). Most horses start to wander a bit because you are playing with the balance beam that is the horse's neck by asking for the change of flexion. The horse may need a bit of time to learn to yield his head without losing his balance. As a rider you have the chance to learn how strong your aids should be so as not to cause your horse to lose his balance. Most riders give their aids too strongly. Using these patterns allows you to think about refining these aids.

Step 3:
Now switch between long and low and a more collected outline and ride a number of transitions.

The same exercise can be ridden on a circle or on an oval. Both of these can be used with canter.

shape to ride and the horse will be forced to straighten and realign his shoulders on the straight sections. In addition, on an oval he has to change his centre of gravity four times rather than keeping it the same, as on a circle.

Developing an internal sense of balance

Until now we have concentrated on putting the horse into a specific situation and allowing him to find his own solution. We have only had to step in when things haven't worked out as we would want – for example when a horse goes too fast on a circle, causing his body to tilt, and then loses his balance. Horses can easily find their own balance, but their balance when being ridden can rarely be developed alone. On a cone circle very few horses will stretch down into a contact with inside flexion – a horse will tend

Dusty flexed to the inside.

Dusty flexed to the outside.

Sciona amidst the S-cones

S-Cones

This is my first choice of exercise when I need to work on the position of the horse's shoulders and hips. You will need to form a serpentine or S-shape with the cones for you to ride through.

Step 1:
Inside flexion. Ride the S with inside flexion. At the point that you change the flexion you will notice that most horses will lose the contact and lift their head up slightly. Practise this until the horse can work through the S without this reaction. The cones will help to prevent the horse from leaning too much on his shoulder.

Step 2:
Outside flexion. Now ride the S with outside flexion. At the change of rein, again, nearly all horses will try to fall out sideways through their quarters to avoid the new positioning. With time a horse should allow his shoulders to be moved over and step forwards through his quarters.

Step 3:
Maintaining flexion. Try to ride through the S maintaining either inside or outside flexion throughout. Your success will depend on the interaction of your aids, because your hands are kept in one position while maintaining the flexion and you have to rely on your other aids (seat and legs) to steer the horse.

Staggered lanes

This obstacle is good for teaching a horse to straighten after lateral movements. He learns neither to transfer his centre of gravity too much to one side nor to fall to one side. Furthermore, as a rider, you will notice how little you need to do to get the horse to move sideways. There are many ways of riding through the lanes, from riding with counter-flexion, through leg yielding to half pass – anything is possible.

The aids will be accepted more willingly because the poles used to form the lanes encourage the horse to go in the given direction.

Baroque circles

This pattern is one of my general-purpose figures to use as soon as a horse is established in his ridden work. It consists of a square whose corners are rounded off, each forming in effect a quarter circle. If you ride the entire figure the horse has to transfer his centre of gravity eight times. Five times around equates, therefore, to forty changes of balance. In comparison, riding

Using staggered lanes teaches a horse to 'catch' any drifting to the side himself and not to lean too much on to his shoulder.

a circle five times asks for only one change to a horse's centre of gravity. Owing to the constant change from straight to quarter circles the horse will become supple and collected. The quarter circles may be ridden in very different ways. It is possible to use inside and outside flexion (RW7) or, as in RW2, to use control of the horse's quarters to swing them around. It is especially important to ask the horse to go straight after the turns without leaning on either shoulder.

Figures of eight

Build a straight line between poles 3 to 5 metres in length. After riding through this line add a 10-metre circle with a change of direction. Your horse will learn to go straight after a circle and not to lean too much on one shoulder. When on the circle pay attention to the position of your horse's neck and shoulders. You can also try using a longer straight line, to carry out RW10 better.

The figures and patterns detailed here are those that I use the most, but there is nothing to stop you coming up with your own. Almost every riding lesson can be supported by the use of cones and foam-filled tubes (to form the outsides of the lanes). The horse can be contained better and will more easily complete the exercises with a correct frame. It isn't always possible to get this correct frame at an early stage with your aids alone because the wish to succeed can cause a rider to tense up or allow the horse to develop bad habits. What we can achieve is an early version of the correct frame with greater lightness (because the rider isn't interfering as much). Given that the correct sequence of movements is being imprinted on the horse he will remember them at a later stage, even without the aids.

In addition the rider has a visual guide and can see if the horse is not moving correctly at an earlier stage. She can take action and correct the horse more quickly. The horse can find his internal and external balance more easily, and the rider learns how strongly and for how long to apply an aid while not causing the horse to lose his balance. This becomes particularly obvious on a circle when working in inside and outside flexion. The horse must learn first to let himself be flexed into a position without losing his balance. Often on my courses riders are surprised how much their horses wobble when doing this because they have never seen this quite so clearly before. This training also has a positive effect on calmness, because riding through the various obstacles means that things will be moving constantly out of and into the horse's field of vision. At the same time the horse also has to concentrate hard on the obstacles.

The positive effect of training with movable obstacles is often underestimated. This may in part lie with the fact that you have to understand the background to this work to really appreciate its purpose. Correctly carried out, the effects (as with riding) can be seen quickly. In human sport, proprioception training is a standard tool used from rehabilitation to high-performance sport. For this reason the correct execution of the exercises is crucial. Setting out just any object, riding in and out, and applying the aids either incorrectly or too strongly, thus causing your horse to lose his balance, is going to be counterproductive. If you let a horse do his own thing in the wrong way over a long period of time over a certain obstacle he will have learnt to do it incorrectly, and it will take even more work to reverse the process.

Sciona turning. She is accepting the hand, is active through her quarters and is concentrating on her work.

After the turn she has straightened up well and is in a lovely outline.

Additional influences on balance

The rider's aids

In an ideal world, the aids should, from the start, help to maintain the horse's balance (like training wheels). Later they will no longer passively offer support but will influence the horse in such a way that he can move his own centre of gravity easily and allow himself to be shaped and directed. A part of this is that the horse should accept the aids willingly. Every pull on the rein or kick of the leg will cause the horse to lose his balance, or will force him to change his balance to deal with the external forces.

On the other hand, a poorly balanced horse will not be able to accept the aids willingly because he can't balance himself. This creates a real dilemma. I need to use my aids to balance the horse, but the horse can't accept them because he isn't balanced.

The solution again lies in knowing the right measures to take. The worse a horse's balance, the less I should actively step in, but the more I will need to use visual aids and support. A round pen (no corners) with lots of in-hand work is the ideal way of dealing with young or unbalanced horses.

Speed

Opinions differ over the correct speed. Some believe that a high speed can in effect 'straighten' out a horse. But let's think about what happens to us when we try to balance on a beam.

If we go too slowly we will start to wobble about and will fall off. If we run, it gets worse. Each one of us will find our own speed that works

best for us. I personally believe that this applies to horses as well. A certain speed will even out any wobbles. This can best be seen in a horse that paces (when instead of diagonal opposites the legs on each side move together). A horse cannot stand on just the two legs on the same side and has to follow quickly with the pair of legs on the other side. Out of necessity this causes a certain speed. The same applies to the normal gaits. This might also be a reason why some horses are perceived as pushy or dominant in walk.

Many horses tend to let their bodies fall forwards, and are constantly running after their centre of gravity in order to avoid falling over. Owing to this 'falling forwards' a certain speed builds up, which can then lead to pushing, especially if the handler is slower. I see horses like this on my courses again and again and my first exercise is always to start to lead the horse as if in slow motion – step by step. Using the exercise that asks the horse to move one leg forwards and then back again is appropriate in this situation as well. A horse will begin to put his leg underneath his body and become better balanced. After five minutes there are no more signs of pushing.

You can therefore see that apparent dominance (the horse won't stop, he is pushy or won't listen to the leg) is often connected with poor balance. Slow motion work in-hand, especially back and forth movement and leg yielding, are all good exercises to improve balance.

If you allow a horse to find his own speed, it is usually the right one. When I move down to walk, I like to let a horse do this.

Other horses, however, race faster and faster. They are running to catch up with their centre of gravity, in other words trying to even out their lack of balance by leaning into corners. When I can see that they are getting faster and more and more frantic it is better to slow them down and start over again. Sometimes a smaller circle may help them to go more slowly, but you do just have to try. Every horse has his own way of dealing with balance problems. In trot, I never push a horse faster at the start, especially in circles or voltes.

Going in a straight line at a certain speed can cause a horse to place his feet closer together. If you watch out for any unsteadiness or swaying, it is easy to establish whether this applies to your own horse. Horses with a poor sense of balance do use speed to avoid falling over. Only a balanced horse can cope without speed. It is up to the rider to feel which speed is suitable for which situation.

Surface

The surface must be non-slip, especially for horses with balance problems. Muddy fields and slippery surfaces are totally unsuitable for working on.

Stress

Balance is also a matter of nerves. It is an undisputed fact that stress can interfere with coordination and balance. Without a degree of inner calmness and relaxation there is not a lot of point in training, and even the way that you handle your horse has an effect. It is not just a matter of education. Training, handling and good communication are the beginnings of balance, because through this means the level of stress will be reduced.

General rules when working with obstacles

The more unbalanced the horse, the more guidance he will require (for example through the use of cones on circles or similar). The handler needs to try and stay as passive as possible. Only during the balance phase of training should you start to ride more actively. The obstacles should be used to influence the way a horse moves, rather than to teach him specific patterns. Make the obstacles fit the relative stage of training the horse is at, and pay attention to the correct distance between you and the horse. On straight lines ask for a long and low contact. Only in advanced stages of balance training should you be asking the horse for collection on straight lines.

Frequently asked questions

When should I ride the exercises?

If you follow this programme you will need about 30 minutes for the warm-up and two exercises. Following this I would then ride either the appropriate applied exercises or the patterns shown. If you get stuck at any stage, I would go back to the relevant foundation exercise. Otherwise the problem might lie in the way the exercise is being executed, so I would work on this. I would always give the horse a break on a long rein after five minutes.

Muscles can't work for a long time without tiring. I work on fitness later, but only when the horse can work in a long and low outline. Once the horse can do individual exercises I would work through these as part of the warm-up because it isn't necessary to ask him repeatedly to do the things he can do well. Restrict the introduction of new exercises to a maximum of two per session, allowing a gap between them. Otherwise you will confuse the horse and he will learn more slowly. Each training session shouldn't be longer than 45 to 50 minutes.

A typical training session

My horse is saddled and I would normally warm him up in-hand using the exercise HE2 on a small circle and by asking him to move his quarters over in walk. I would use CE2 to check that my horse's attention is focused on me. After that I would bring him back to halt for a moment (CE1) and move on to CE5 and CE6. If he does this well then I would get on him and let him stand for 30 seconds or so and then continue to warm up in walk and trot. I check that the basics are all there and will then move on to the exercises for the day.

This process helps me to concentrate and prepare the horse for his work. I always think about what I am doing and how I am going to do it beforehand and try to stick to this. Only by doing this do you remain in control and you will not just react to what the horse happens to be doing.

Between exercises

As already mentioned, I only work on each exercise for a few minutes at a time. What do I do in between? In the foundation module I like to let the horse stand still or let him walk on long rein. I am always trying to work towards internal and external relaxation and looseness so taking lots of pauses works well. When the horse can trot in a long and low outline, this is also a good way to fill the gaps.

In the collection and shoulder module we should have reached this state of relaxedness, but work on the horse's strength will become more important. This is why I switch between sections of walk, followed by trot on a long contact, and collected canter, because this is a good way of loosening and building muscle strength.

Speed

The tempo in walk should be such that the horse's head swings gently back and forth. I let the horse choose his own speed so that I don't have to use my legs continuously. It is common that in the exercises the horse will slow down, but this resolves itself in time.

More significant is the speed in trot. Most horses are ridden too fast and then have problems balancing. It is crucial that the horse stretches down into the contact because then he can be worked effectively. Horses that are not soft through their backs will not work harder by going fast – they will just get faster. The speed should be such that you can go sitting, because it is hard to keep a light contact through the reins when you are rising.

Sitting or rising trot?

My experience has shown me that horses respond much better to the aids when I go sitting. The ridden exercises should always be done sitting, although during the warm-up you may find rising or a more forward seat to be better. You will, however, have to use rising trot if you can't sit to your horse's trot.

Style of riding

The ability of a horse to learn has nothing to do with the style you ride him in (whether Western, English or something else) or how the horse is kept. It is all about trying to explain to the horse in the simplest way possible what you want him to do. If you understand the principles involved in training then there should be no problems in training a horse according to the demands of any particular way or style of riding.

Rideability and calmness are qualities universally desired of a horse.

Duration of the modules

The foundation module generally takes three months to work through (refer to page 52). It is difficult to give a duration for the remaining modules because the prerequisites are different. In the case of the collection and shoulder module, the ability of a horse to carry himself plays a decisive role, because in order to free up the shoulder the horse has to be able to

carry more weight through his quarters. In this module therefore the horse's physical development is the deciding factor. The exercises themselves are learnt by most horses within two months; however, it takes another three to four months for the horse to develop physically. Within therefore a total of six months the emphasis will move from doing the exercises to actually riding, although I would still maintain the use of interval training. After five minutes of canter any horse will need a break. At this stage, when you are gradually building up work, it is important not to lose any of the horse's relaxedness and for this reason I use the module concentrating on the hips and neck to avoid any issues of stiffness or tension.

The speed with which a horse completes the calmness module successfully depends to a great extent on the individual horse and his experience. Some horses are naturally laid back, while others are hot or nervy and need more time. Similar differences exist with regard to the degree to which a horse can coordinate his movement, which is why here too I can't give you exact timings. In the work to build on the initial module, though, I like to use the obstacles because these show up issues faster and help to keep horse and rider in the right frame. Training will then become clearly more effective.

Safety

Even when you are prepared to wait for the right reaction to happen, it is all too easy for a horse to get either overexcited or upset. If you are standing in front of a horse holding his reins and you feel that he is going to rear, let go. Safety of horse and rider is almost the most important thing.

Equipment

Sturdy footwear (in some circumstances safety boots with steel toecaps) and gloves should always be used as a matter of course. A riding hat to an appropriate safety standard is recommended even when it isn't part of the standard equipment in some styles of riding. Apart from this the equipment used should be suitable for the demands being placed on it. I prefer, for example, lead ropes that are about 4 metres long because I can then let the horse move further away from me if necessary. If you have ever had a rearing horse at the other end of your rope you will know that a 1-metre rope is a bit short. The halter is of secondary importance as long as the horse can't get out of it.

In the balance module I use flexible poles (covered foam pads) in order to reduce the risk of a horse hurting himself. When you are using the poles to form a lane along which the horse is walking, the risk is too high that the horse might stand on a pole and pull a tendon.

Final steps

How do I tell my horse what I would like him to do?

What do I actually want to tell him?

These thoughts started it all. I hope that I have been able to answer the first question. Thinking about learning behaviour has nothing to do with riding, but is a necessity that has to become part of your thought processes as a rider. All too often fundamentals are justified by referring to the ways and customs of a particular way of riding. 'You have to do

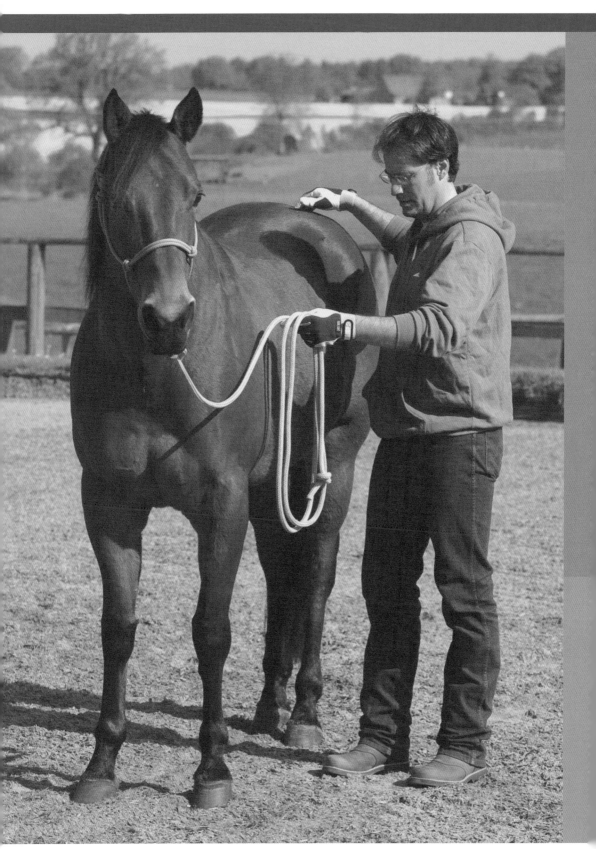

it this way' is a much-loved phrase to give a reason for something for which there is no reason. If you start to question things and look at riding from a different angle, then I have achieved what I hoped to do.

Only you can determine the 'what'. I have developed the content of my training programme from my point of view. When I think of my ideal horse I imagine a general utility type of horse. This term comes from the riding style used with working horses. Horses used for work have to be easy to ride, have strong nerves and be able to carry out their work well, even if you aren't riding them continuously on the aids. To put it another way: Today I would like to be able to ride a medium dressage test and tomorrow I would like to be able to load up my horse and take him off on a long ride. These demands require a horse to have certain qualities. Many of these are already determined by the horse's own character, but every disposition can be influenced by careful and targeted training. None of the modules can stand alone – they are all intertwined with each other. A horse with poor balance will not be able to respond well to the aids and will get more nervous. A horse that has learned to go against the hand will cause himself to lose his balance. Compare training a horse to juggling – the individual modules are the balls and it is our job to keep everything in sight and not to fix too much attention on one area. The field of biodynamics is particularly interesting. A horse is a complex being (and not just in a physical sense) that has to move in a particular way in order fulfil his role and stay healthy. You could say that the individual parts of his body are the adjusting screws that we can have an influence on, and our aids are the screw-drivers. At the same time, though, you must explain the aids to the horse beforehand and take his emotions into consideration. By looking at things this way you are creating a base for the training of horse and rider. All of a sudden we can see new solutions in certain areas that have never occurred to us before and that may cause a total change of direction.

Thies Böttcher

Thanks

I would like to thank everyone who has supported me in making this book a reality – especially the following people:

Britta Kutscher can be seen in the photos riding Sciona but has also made sure that all the horses were in shape from an osteopathic point of view. For years she has explained patiently to me what is happening physiologically to the horses during our work. Without her my programme would today look quite different.

I would like to thank Christian Schütz for providing me with photographic equipment.

I owe a large vote of thanks to Henning Ramm because he allowed me to use his wonderful facilities when taking the photos.

A big thank you to Iris Ramen for letting me use Dusty for so many of the pictures.

I would also like to mention the team at Cadmos. Thank you for your professional support and the trust placed in this book.

Last but not least, I would like to thank my partner Birgit. She gave me the opportunity to do the things I needed to do, read my manuscript innumerable times, took part in the photo shoots (with Lilly) and was the friendly ghost in the background who took care of everything.

Further reading

Becker, Horst:
The Athletic Horse
Cadmos Books, 2010

Böttcher, Thies:
GHT-Online Journal
www.gentle-horse-training.de

Heuschmann, Gerd:
Tug of War: Classical Versus Modern Dressage
J.A. Allen, 2007

Schmelzer, Angelika:
Horse Behaviour Explained
Cadmos Books, 2002

Weritz, Linda:
Horse Sense and Horsemanship
Cadmos Books, 2006

Addresses

Britta Kutscher
Osteopathische Pferdetherapie
Fischerstraße 7
D-24972 Steinberg (bei Flensburg)
Tel: 0049 4632 7973
www.physiokutscher.de

Christian Schütz
Flex-KS
Schwalbenstr. 4
D-91154 Roth
Tel: 0049 9171 981686
www.pferde-bodenarbeit.de

Pferdehof Ramm
Ringstrasse 15a
D-23845 Grabau
Tel: 0049 4537 1357
www.pferdehof-ramm.de

Snike Sport GmgH
Königsalle 57
D-71638 Ludwigsburg
Tel: 0049 7141 916 6560
www.snaix.com

Birgit Hencke
www.animalcurare.de

Thies Böttcher
www.gentle-horse-training.de
Tel: 0049 179 204 1368

Index

CADMOS
HORSE BOOKS

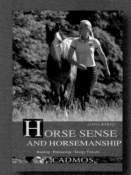

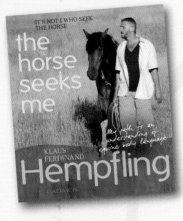

Klaus Ferdinand Hempfling
THE HORSE SEEKS ME

In this lavishly illustrated book, Klaus Ferdinand Hempfling explains his system of communicating naturally with the instincts and nature of horses. The reader follows the progress of Arab stallion Marouk, and Lusitano stallion Queijo, in discovering a confident and harmonious relationship with their rider. Giving comprehensive insight into Hempfling's methods, the horses' progress is documented step-by-step, uncovering old wounds in the process that have resulted in their difficult behaviour. Readers will discover the fascinating process of understanding horses through the fine art of body language.

352 pages
Softcover with French folds, full colour
ISBN 978-3-86127-975-4

Linda Weritz
HORSE SENSE AND HORSEMANSHIP

This book explores how mutual trust and respec form the basis of a fulfilling partnership. Every horse needs a trustworthy leader. A rider in who the horse has no confidence forces the animal to take charge. As soon as a rider understands this balance of power, he or she can establish a sma herd relationship as the basis for a successful partnership, leading to a true friendship with their equine companion.

128 pages
Softcover, full colour
ISBN 978-3-86127-928-0

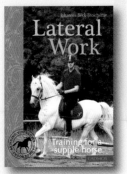

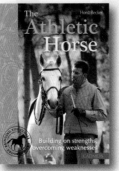

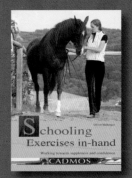

Johannes Beck-Broichsitter
LATERAL WORK

Lateral work is an essential part of any training programme leading to a supple horse. This book offers a step-by-step guide through all of the lateral movements, introducing exercises to prepare horse and rider for the first lateral movements, through to training exercises, as well as stretching and loosening exercises.

128 pages
Softcover, full colour
ISBN 978-3-86127-973-0

Horst Becker
THE ATHLETIC HORSE

When problems occur during a horse's dressage training, all too often the question 'Why?' is ignored. In this book, Horst Becker endeavours to find answers to this question. Whilst demonstrating ways in which a horse's weaknesses can be systematically corrected, he also shows quiet and effective ways of developing its strengths.

144 pages
Softcover, full colour
ISBN 978-3-86127-976-1

Oliver Hilberger
SCHOOLING EXERCISES IN-HAND

This book explains step-by-step and with clea illustrations the straightforward way towards the correct training of horses, working from the ground. Particular emphasis is given to th description of lateral movements, which for a supple horse as well as for the preparation towards the more advanced movements, play central role.

160 pages
Softcover, full colour
ISBN 978-3-86127-964-8

For more information, please visit
www.cadmos.co.uk

CADMOS